BY THE EDITORS OF CONSUMER GUIDE

D0602566

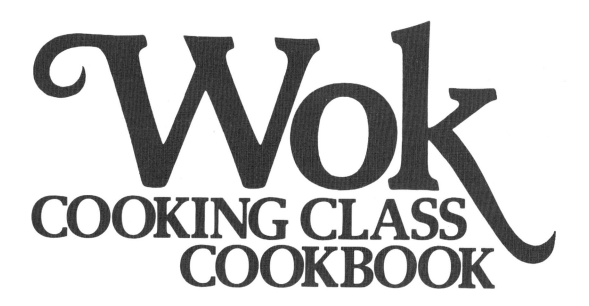

Wok
COOKING CLASS
COOKBOOK

Publications International, Ltd.

Contents

Library of Congress Catalog Card Number: 83-62115
ISBN 1-56173-458-6

On the Front Cover: Velvet Shrimp
On the Back Cover: Crisp-Fried Crescents, Curry Fried Rice, Soup of
    Sole and Vegetables, and Double-Fried Pork Strips

Recipe Testing and Editing: Suzanne Checchia.
Original Recipes by: Osamu Harrada, Kijun Ohma and Sachlyo Usuda.
Arranged by: Gakken Co., Ltd., Tokyo, Japan.
Cover Design: Linda Shum.

Printed in USA

Introduction

To the Chinese, food is seen as much more than simple nourishment' for the body. Dishes are designed with a balance of contrasting and complementary colors, textures, flavors and shapes. Such diversity adds to the richness and challenge of exploring Chinese cuisine, providing an exciting path to new culinary experiences.

A unifying link between the regional cuisines is the use of the wok as the primary cooking vessel. The wok evolved centuries ago along with specialized cooking techniques in response to fuel-poor, labor-rich conditions. Designed with rounded shape and long sloping sides, it provides an extended cooking surface which can be heated to very high temperatures with little fuel. It is most commonly associated with the technique of stir-frying, but is versatile enough to be used to deep-fry, steam, simmer and shallow-fry.

Recipes in this book highlight the unique versatility of the wok. Included are basic cooking processes, as well as the techniques of pretreating ingredients, such as marinating, coating, velveting, tenderizing and cutting. They include hot and cold dishes, spicy and mild dishes and an array of color, shape and texture combinations.

The servings recommended at the end of each recipe are based on the Western eating style, where one entree is served with rice, a salad and/or vegetable and perhaps a soup. If serving a meal Chinese-style, they will go a bit further.

A Chinese-style meal is generally composed of 3 or 4 main dishes plus rice and a soup. Dim sum, small portions of food served as appetizers or as a light snack might precede the meal, although, when larger portions are served, dim sum can become a light luncheon or dinner meal. When selecting dishes for a Chinese meal, take into consideration such elements as textures, flavors and colors. A whole meal of stir-frys, for example, would be monotonous, as would one consisting entirely of highly spicy foods or all soft-textured foods.

Both novice and experienced cooks will find the following sections on equipment, techniques and ingredients helpful. Read them before trying the recipes. Then begin the exciting adventure of cooking with your wok.

THE WOK AND OTHER EQUIPMENT

Woks are available in many different styles, sizes, materials and prices. The traditional wok is made of rolled steel which conducts heat evenly and responds readily to temperature changes so that it heats up and cools down quickly. It is heavy enough for stability and to prevent scorching but not so heavy that it is cumbersome. It can be rinsed immediately after cooking without warping. Woks are also made of carbon steel, stainless steel, aluminum and copper but none combine all the properties of rolled steel.

Woks come in sizes from 12 to 24 inches. The 14-inch size is the most versatile and practical for home cooking. It has a large enough volume and will fit on most range tops without blocking other burners. A wok should have high sloping sides for stir-frying and enough depth for safe deep-frying. Wok handles have either 2 metal loops positioned opposite each other on the rim or 1 loop and 1 long conventional handle. To prevent burns and eliminate the need for pot holders, loops and handles covered with wood are preferred. Other types of woks available are the flat-bottomed wok that is designed for use on electric or smooth-surface ranges, and the electric wok which sometimes has a nonstick surface. Although the electric wok does not allow for the quick temperature adjustment often needed in stir-frying, it is acceptable for deep-frying, steaming and simmering.

Essential wok accessories include a ring or collar which sits securely on top of the range around the burner. The ring holds the round-bottomed wok in a stable position. A ring with sloping sides allows you to set the wok in the larger opening, placing it closer to the flame, when you want intense heat, or in the smaller opening, further from the flame, when you need to slow simmer. A tight-fitting domed wok cover, usually made of lightweight aluminum, is another necessity. It should be slightly smaller in diameter than your wok so that it fits just inside the upper perimeter of the wok.

A new steel wok must be seasoned before using. Seasoning is a permanent layer of hardened oil that is applied initially and continues to build as the wok is used. It prevents the wok from rusting between uses, prevents sticking and allows food to move properly during stir-frying with a minimum use of oil.

To season, scour the wok thoroughly to remove any protective coating, rinse well and dry thoroughly. Heat the wok over high heat until very hot; add 2 tablespoons vegetable oil and swirl to coat the inside of the wok. Heat until the oil begins to smoke, about one minute. Turn off the heat and rub the oil into the entire inner surface with a thick pad of folded paper toweling. Cool the wok 5 minutes and wipe out any visible oil. Repeat this process several times, using fresh oil and the same paper toweling each time, until the center area of the wok becomes blackened. Immediately after the last application, wipe off all traces of oil with clean paper toweling so the wok will not be sticky when cool. The black seasoned area will increase with repeated use of the wok and will eventually cover the entire inner surface.

To maintain the seasoned surface, never wash a wok with soap. Simply fill with hot water and rub with a sponge. The wok is most easily cleaned right after cooking while it is still hot. For tough food particles use a soft-bristled brush or plastic scrubber, but never use a metal scouring pad. Dry the wok immediately. Before storing the wok, heat it over high heat briefly, rub with a teaspoon of oil and cool. Store in a dry place.

Stir-Frying Implements. Two tools commonly used in stir-frying are the Chinese spatula or shovel and the ladle or scoop. The working end of the spatula is a wide flared piece of metal with a rounded edge that conforms to the shape of the wok; the ladle has a broad bowl shape. The tools are used together: the spatula for stirring and tossing, the ladle for adding liquid ingredients and basting. Together they are used to quickly scoop cooked food out of the wok. The ladle is not essential and other appropriate long-handled instruments can be substituted for the spatula. Long cooking chopsticks are an alternative, but require skill and dexterity. The Western slotted or solid metal spatula or a flat wooden or bamboo spatula can also be used.

Strainer. The Chinese mesh strainer is made of fine wire woven in a wide shallow bowl-shape attached to a bamboo handle. It is ideal for deep-frying and velveting. The handle does not conduct heat and the wide skimming surface is useful for turning food, removing food from the wok and draining over the wok. A suitable alternative is the wide Western strainer made of perforated metal. A conventional slotted spoon can also be used.

Deep-Fat Thermometer. An accurate deep-fat thermometer is essential for deep-frying and velveting. It should clip on the side of the wok, or rest stably on the edge so both hands remain free and the thermometer does not interfere with proper circulation of the food.

Steaming Equipment. The Chinese bamboo steamer consists of round stacking baskets and a lid. The baskets are about 3½ inches deep with a base of bamboo strips woven together in an open network; the lids are tightly woven with no spaces. Since they come in a wide range of diameters, find one that will fit snugly inside your wok, resting about 1 inch below the edge. For example, a 14-inch wok needs 12-inch baskets. The pieces are sold separately and a basic set-up of 2 baskets and 1 lid will fill most needs.

Chinese Chopping Block. This is a cross section of a tree trunk, about 16 inches across and 5 or 6 inches thick. Sturdy and porous, it can withstand heavy chopping and the blows of a cleaver. The blocks are not widely available, and for most purposes, a sturdy cutting board or a thick butcher block will work.

Chinese Cleaver. Cleavers are available in various weights with the medium weight being an acceptable general-purpose weight. It is a multipurpose tool useful not only for slicing; the flat side can be used for pounding vegetables and meats, and the handle for grinding spices in a bowl.

WOK COOKING METHODS

Stir-Frying. The cooking method most identified with Chinese cuisine is stir-frying, the brisk cooking of ingredients in a small amount of oil over intense heat for a short time. This intense heat source must be capable of instant adjustment and control. For this reason, gas heat is the easiest and most efficient to use. Good stir-frying can be done on an electric range if measures are taken to accommodate for its slow responsiveness.

One method is to use two preheated burners, one set on the highest heat and the second set at low or medium. Simply switch the wok back and forth as the recipe requires. Another alternative when only brief periods of lower heat are required is to lift the wok off the high heat and set it down on a cool part of the range or in a second wok ring on a nearby counter. The heat of the wok should be high enough to provide a few seconds of low- or medium-heat cooking. Return the wok to the hot burner and proceed. The recipes in this book were developed on a gas range and some slight

adjustments in timing may be necessary if you are using an electric range.

Successful stir-frying is broken down into two separate parts: preparing the ingredients and the actual cooking. The first phase requires the most time and labor; the second phase is very brief and must proceed quickly and uninterrupted.

Preparation: Read the recipe from start to finish. Prepare *all* ingredients ahead of time. Follow cutting dimensions exactly; they are tailored to the nature of the ingredient as well as the dish and are critical in ensuring that all ingredients will reach the proper state of doneness when stir-frying is complete. *Stir-frying proceeds so quickly that once it begins there is no time to stop and cut or measure ingredients.*

Assemble all measured and prepared ingredients in the order they will be added within reach near the cooking area. Solid ingredients can be placed in separate piles on a large working platter or in individual small bowls assembled on a large tray. Assemble all utensils, plates and paper toweling that will be needed. Place the serving dish or bowl in a 200°F oven to preheat.

Stir-frying: Place wok in its ring over the burner. Turn the heat to highest setting; heat wok until very hot, 15 to 30 seconds. A drop of water in the wok should sizzle and evaporate instantly when the wok is hot enough. *If wok is not properly preheated, ingredients will tend to stick.* Add oil in wide circle about ⅓ of the way down from top edge of wok, letting it flow down the sides to bottom. Lift wok and swirl the oil to coat the lower ⅔ of the inner surface. Heat oil over high heat until hot, about 30 seconds longer.

In the first cooking step, the aromatic ingredients, such as ginger, green onion, garlic and chili peppers are added to the hot oil and cooked briefly over reduced heat to develp their aroma and to flavor the oil.

In the second step, the main ingredients are added in a logical sequence and quickly seared. The ingredients are gradually added, often being "showered" or "scattered" in from above with one hand, while the other hand briskly stirs and tosses them with the cooking spatula. The fast tossing motion ensures that every surface of the food is quickly coated and seared with hot oil to seal in the natural juices and flavorings. If ingredients are added too quickly and in too large a quantity, the oil and pan temperature will drop drastically; the food will simmer and steam, becoming dry, tough or limp before the heat recovers.

The third step involves adding the major liquids and seasonings which have usually been combined in a bowl. The liquid is poured in a wide circle around the inside of the wok so that it begins to heat as it flows down the sides. It is quickly stirred in and brought to boiling. Any final cooking is then done, either uncovered for a brief simmer, or covered for a brief steam-cooking.

The final step includes the addition of cornstarch for thickening if appropriate. Any final seasonings and perhaps a bit of oil for glossing are added and stirred very briefly just to lightly incorporate. The food is transferred to the preheated serving dish and served immediately. *The carefully balanced textures and consistency of a stir-fried dish are at their peak at this moment; they will deteriorate if the food is held.*

Deep-Frying. Almost as prevalent in Chinese cuisine as stir-frying, deep-frying lends a variety of appearances, tastes and textures to a Chinese meal. The wok, ideally suited for deep-frying, will maintain an even oil temperature without burning and is deep enough to accommodate large pieces of food. Its wide diameter and rounded shape reduce the amount of oil needed to fry a large quantity of smaller pieces. For best results, follow these guidelines.

Heat the wok over high heat until very hot, about 20 seconds. *If the wok is not preheated before oil is added, the food will tend to stick.* Add the oil to the wok and heat to the specified temperature, using a deep-fat thermometer for accuracy.

The key to successful deep-frying is to maintain the oil temperature. Food should be at room temperature before adding. It is added gradually and fried in batches so the oil temperature does not drop drastically. If the temperature is lowered too much, the coating will not set properly, the batter will become oil-soaked and the food will become tough and greasy.

When adding moist foods such as uncoated chicken or large pieces of food such as whole fish to the oil, hold the wok cover over one side as a shield against spattering. Cooked food must be quickly removed from the oil with a strainer or slotted spoon and drained on paper toweling. Serve at once before the food becomes soggy.

The Chinese often fry batter-coated foods in two stages. The first stage sets the batter and starts the cooking; the second finishes the cooking and crisps and colors the coating. Between stages, the food continues to cook in its own heat and some of the moisture in the batter evaporates, allowing it to become crisper in the final frying.

Oil used for deep-frying can be saved for another use. Simply cool the oil and strain into a clean container; cover and refrigerate. Add about ⅓ cup fresh oil to each ⅔ cup of the reserved oil the next time you fry.

Steaming. Steaming is a highly valued method of Chinese cooking. It preserves and intensifies the pure natural flavors and colors of foods. The steam envelopes the food, providing a steady penetrating heat which allows the food to cook and baste in its own juices. For best results, follow these guidelines.

Line a bamboo steamer basket with a plate, a clean wet cloth or cabbage or lettuce leaves as directed in the recipe; arrange food in the basket. Place basket in wok. Add boiling water to wok, pouring it down the side, to a level 1 inch below bottom of basket; turn heat to high. Cover the basket. Keep extra boiling water handy.

Steam the food as directed in the recipe. Some dishes require vigorous steam, others mild. In any case, it must be steady, not intermittent. If using more than one steamer basket, reverse their positions occasionally for even cooking. Check the water level frequently during steaming and replenish if necessary with additional boiling water. When the food is done, turn off the heat. Carefully remove the basket from the wok. Let stand a few seconds to allow heat to dissipate before uncovering.

Caution: Steam heat is very intense. When checking the water level, checking the food for doneness or changing basket positions, protect hands with cooking mitts or towels. When lifting the lid, open it away from you; never put your face too close to the steam.

CHINESE CUTTING TECHNIQUES

Several cutting techniques common in Chinese cookery are designed to ensure proper cooking time and maximum flavor benefits, as well as provide interesting shapes and textures. The Chinese use the multipurpose cleaver almost exclusively, but all of these techniques can be done with Western knives. Use the tool with which you are more comfortable and concentrate on precision cutting, one of the keys to successful wok cookery.

Slant-Cut. Used to obtain slices that are longer than the dimensions of the ingredient alone would allow. This may be desirable to expose more surface area for faster cooking and flavor penetration or simply to provide a more interesting appearance. It is often used with flat thin pieces of meat or poultry and long thin vegetables.

Hold the cleaver crosswise above the ingredient and at an angle to it and the cutting board; slice downward following the angle. Repeat to cut slices of uniform thickness. The degree of the angle determines the length of the slice. For most purposes the cleaver is held at a 30° to 45° angle. If you want to shave off very thin, very long slices, hold cleaver at a sharp angle, almost horizontal to the board.

Diagonal-Cut. Used primarily to cut long thin vegetables into oval slices, or in the case of celery, elongated crescents. The diagonal-cut exposes more surface area than the conventional straight slice and provides a pleasing shape.

Hold the cleaver perpendicular to the board but at an angle to the ingredient; slice straight downward. Repeat to cut slices of uniform thickness.

Roll-Cut. A variation of the simple diagonal cut. This specialty cut is most often used on long and/or fibrous vegetables such as carrots, asparagus and bamboo shoots. It is another method of exposing more surface area, in a chunky, irregular form. Although the angles are irregularly placed, the overall dimensions of the pieces should be consistent for even cooking.

Hold cleaver perpendicular to board but at a moderate angle to the ingredient. Cut ¾ to 1½ inches off the end with a diagonal cut. Roll the ingredient a quarter to a third of a turn away from you. Cut again at the same angle and at an equal distance down the length. Repeat rolling and cutting.

Slant-Cut: Hold cleaver crosswise to ingredient and at angle to it and cutting board; slice downward following angle.

Diagonal-Cut: Hold cleaver at angle to ingredient and perpendicular to cutting board; slice straight downward.

Roll-Cut: Make diagonal cut; roll ingredient a quarter or a third turn away from you; repeat diagonal cut.

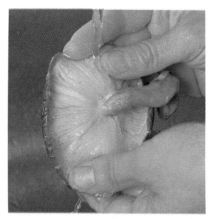

Dried Mushrooms: Add boiling water to mushrooms in heatproof bowl (left). After soaking, rinse under cold water and rub gently to release sand and grit (center). Snip off tough fibrous stems (right).

SPECIAL PREPARATION TECHNIQUES

To Soften and Clean Dried Black Chinese Mushrooms. Place mushrooms in small heatproof bowl; add enough boiling water to cover mushrooms. Let stand until mushrooms have rehydrated to their original size and are soft and supple, about 30 minutes.

Remove mushrooms from water. Rinse individually under cold running water, rubbing cap gently between thumbs and fingertips to loosen and release any sand or grit that may be trapped in the cap.

Snip off and discard the tough fibrous stems with scissors or cut off with paring knife. Squeeze mushrooms firmly between palms to remove excess water which would dilute the flavor of the recipe. Mushrooms are ready to use, or they can be refrigerated, wrapped in plastic wrap, up to 12 hours.

The soaking liquid contains good mushroom flavor and is sometimes reserved for use in the recipe. In this case, strain the liquid through a sieve lined with a double thickness of cheesecloth. Otherwise discard soaking liquid.

To Soften and Clean Dried Cloud Ears. Place cloud ears in small heatproof bowl; add 1 cup boiling water. Although dried cloud ears look very small, they swell when soaked and require proportionally much more water than dried black mushrooms for softening. Let stand until cloud ears have expanded and are soft and springy, 20 to 30 minutes.

Drain cloud ears, discarding soaking water. Rinse cloud ear pieces individually under cold water, rubbing pieces be-

tween thumbs and fingertips to loosen and release any bits of wood or other debris that may be trapped in the folds.

Drain cloud ears well. Pinch off and discard the hard "eye" at the base of separate petals or the thick tough portion at the base of clusters. Pat with paper toweling to remove excess water. Cloud ears are ready to use, or they can be refrigerated, wrapped in plastic wrap, up to 12 hours.

Pounding with Cleaver. Used on fresh ginger root slices and green onions to break up the fibers enough so they will release flavoring juices.

Place pared ginger slices or trimmed green onions in single layer on cutting board. Tap or pound with a quick, light stroke of the broad flat side of cleaver. Use enough force to flatten the pieces slightly without splitting them completely apart. If you do not have a cleaver, use the smooth side of a meat mallet. This technique, applied with greater force, is also used to flatten boneless pieces of meat or poultry to uniform thickness.

March-Chop. Used to loosen and lighten the compact texture of ground meats so they combine evenly in stuffings and quickly separate into fine pieces when stir-fried.

Place meat on cutting board and press into a pile about 1-inch thick. Hold cleaver perpendicular to board and chop through meat at about ⅛-inch intervals, chopping from one end of the meat to the other. Slide cleaver under pile of meat; lift up and flip the meat over in one piece. Holding cleaver perpendicular to board and at right angle to the first set of cuts, chop through pile of meat as before.

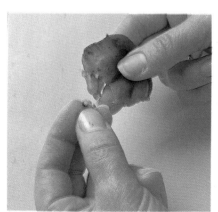

Dried Cloud Ears: Add boiling water to cloud ears in heatproof bowl (left). After soaking, rinse under cold water and rub gently to remove wood and other debris (center). Pinch off hard "eye" at base of petals (right).

March-Chop: Press ground meat into 1-inch thick pile on cutting board (left). Chop through meat at 1/8-inch intervals (center). Slide cleaver under meat; lift and turn over in one piece (right). Chop again at right angle to first set of cuts.

GLOSSARY OF CHINESE INGREDIENTS

Baby corn (also called young corn): 2 to 3-inch long yellow ears of corn with tiny kernels and fully edible cobs are slightly sweet tasting and crunchy; used for color and texture in stir-frys and soups and for garnish. Available in cans packed in salted water; drain and rinse with cold water to remove brine before using. Store unused corn covered with water in jar in refrigerator 1 week to 10 days; change water every 2 days.

Bamboo shoots: tender shoots of the tropical bamboo plant have a faint sweetness and slight crispness and range in color from ivory to pale yellow. The whole shoot is cone-shaped with a thick compact outer wall and an open network at the core. Available in cans packed in water in several forms, including long thin whole shoots, short stocky cone-shaped tips, halves, long thick wedges and thin slices. Drain and rinse well before using. Store covered with cold water in jar in refrigerator 2 to 3 weeks; change water every 2 days.

Bamboo shoots, young (also called green or spring): these young shoots are more delicate and tender than the more mature shoots. They are often used in red-cooked or other simmered dishes. Rinse and store as for regular shoots.

Bean curd (also called tofu or dow foo): made from soybeans, bean curd is pure white in color and has the consistency of firm custard. Available fresh in approximately 3-inch cakes with either straight or rounded edges, weighing about 1 pound. Chinese-style bean curd is firmer and sturdier than Japanese bean curd and is preferred for the recipes in this book. Rinse and drain well before using. Store covered with water in refrigerator up to 1 week; change water daily.

Bean paste, sweetened: made from pureed red beans and sugar. Available in cans. Will keep for several weeks refrigerated in covered glass container.

Bean sprouts, mung: long white shoots sprouted from the small green mung bean, the fresh sprouts should be firm, crisp and plump, not limp or shriveled and should be white with pale gold flecks, not brown. They have a fresh clean grassy flavor. Available in 1- or 2-pound plastic bags, they will keep in the refrigerator up to 1 week but are best used immediately. Rinse well before using and remove the dry loose bean husks. Canned mung bean sprouts are available but not recommended.

Bean sprouts, soy: similar to mung bean sprouts, these are sprouted from the larger yellow soybean. The shoots are longer and thicker; the flavor stronger and more beanlike. Treat the same as mung bean sprouts.

Bean threads (also called cellophane or transparent noodles): very thin, white, dried noodles made from mung bean starch. For use in soups and stir-frys they are soaked briefly in hot water, then in cold water before cooking. As they soften, they become transparent. During cooking, the flavorless noodles absorb a large quantity of liquid, taking on the flavors of the foods they are cooked with. Available in tightly folded skeins, bound with rubber bands or string, in packages of various sizes starting at 2 ounces. Will keep indefinitely in tightly covered container in cool dry place.

Black beans, fermented (also called salted black beans): preserved black soybeans with pungent, salty flavor. Used primarily as a seasoning; often rinsed before using to remove excess salt. Available in cans or sealed plastic bags. Will keep indefinitely in tightly covered container in refrigerator.

Brown bean sauce, regular and ground (also called brown bean paste, yellow bean paste or sweet bean sauce): a thick reddish-brown paste with salty, slightly sweet flavor; made from fermented soybeans, salt, flour and water. Regular bean sauce contains whole or slightly mashed beans within the paste; the ground version is a smooth puree. They can be used interchangeably with slight flavor and texture differences. Available in cans and jars; canned bean sauce should be transferred to a jar for storage. Store covered with a thin layer of peanut oil in tightly covered jar in refrigerator; will keep indefinitely.

Cabbage, Chinese pickled: types of pickled cabbage include snow cabbage, napa and celery cabbage. They vary in color from almost white to dark green. Available canned and in sealed plastic pouches in the refrigerated section, pickled cabbage comes in many forms including small whole heads, wedges, shredded and chopped. It should be rinsed or soaked in cold water to remove excess salt before using. Once opened, it can be refrigerated in its brine in a tightly covered glass container for several weeks. Well-rinsed Western sauerkraut can be substituted if necessary.

Celery cabbage: a member of the Chinese cabbage family. The long thin compact head is comprised primarily of thick wide crisp white stem with a small proportion of thin soft pale green leaf. Used in soups, salads, stir-frys, simmered dishes and in fillings for egg rolls and dumplings. Refrigerate sealed in plastic bag up to 1 week.

Chili peppers, dried red: essential to many Szechuanese and other spicy dishes, these fiery-hot peppers are bright red, 2 to 3 inches long and 1/4 to 1/2 inch thick. The seeds are the hottest part and are often removed and discarded. (*Caution*: the oils in the peppers can cause skin burns. When handling peppers, be careful not to touch face or eyes; wash hands immediately afterward.) Available in sealed cellophane bags; will keep indefinitely tightly covered in cool, dark, dry place. Dried red Spanish chilies or dried red chili flakes can be substituted.

Chili sauce (also called chili paste): bright red in color and thin to medium in consistency, with a clean, fresh, hot flavor. It is made from crushed red chili peppers and salt; some brands include other flavorings such as onion, lemon, sweet potato and vinegar. **Chili sauce with soybean** (also called hot bean paste), is thicker, darker and sometimes saltier. **Chili paste with garlic** is similar to chili sauce but is saltier and has a pronounced garlic flavor. The specific product called for in a recipe should be used if possible, but if necessary, these can be substituted for another with slightly different flavor, texture and color results. Available in cans or jars; will keep indefinitely in tightly covered jar in refrigerator.

Chinese chives (also called garlic chives): a strongly flavored dark green herb with a flavor similar to Western chives plus garlic. The flat leaves are 8 to 12 inches long. Used in soups and stir-frys. Sold seasonally by the bunch in Oriental markets. Refrigerate sealed in plastic bag up to 1 week.

Cloud ears, dried (also called wood ears, tree ears or Judas ears): a dried edible tree fungus with brittle wrinkled texture. Color ranges from pale grayish-tan to black; size varies from thin, small, separate flakes to large, thick, connected clusters. They must be softened and cleaned before using. Upon soaking, they expand into rubbery, slightly cupped petal shapes. Having little flavor of their own, they are used primarily for color and texture. Sold by weight; will keep indefinitely in covered container at room temperature. No substitute; can be omitted if desired.

Coriander (also called Chinese parsley): a pungent aromatic fresh green herb with long stems and thin flat leaves. Sold by the bunch in Oriental food stores and in Latin-American markets where it is called cilantro. Refrigerate loosely wrapped in plastic or with stems immersed in a glass of water and leaves covered with a plastic bag; will keep up to 1 week. No substitute.

Curry sauce (also called curry paste): a spicy, slightly fruity mixture prepared from chili peppers, onion and numerous aromatic spices. It has a cleaner, fresher flavor than curry powder and is preferred in Chinese cooking. Available in cans and jars; will keep indefinitely in tightly covered jar in refrigerator.

Egg roll wrappers (also called egg roll skins): thin sheets of noodle-type dough available in 7 or 8-inch squares or circles. Sold fresh or frozen in sealed plastic bags; look for wrappers which are soft and supple, or if frozen, check to see that the edges are not dried out. Wrappers will keep refrigerated up to 1 week or frozen for 3 months. Thaw in refrigerator overnight. Keep tightly wrapped in plastic until ready to use to prevent drying.

Five-spice powder (also called five-fragrance powder): a brown-colored powdery blend of 5 or more spices, including anise, fennel, cloves, cinnamon, ginger and Szechuan peppercorns. Sold by weight. Store indefinitely in tightly covered jar in cool, dark place.

Ginger root, fresh: a knobby root which grows in plump connected lobes. It has tan skin and gold flesh often tinged with bluish-green. The flavor is clean, fresh and pungent. Ginger is used minced, cut into fine shreds or small squares or into thin slices which are lightly pounded to release their juices. When thin slices are specified in this book, they should be cut about $\frac{1}{16}$-inch thick and 1 inch in diameter. Sold by weight, the knobs should be very hard, not spongy, with firm smooth skin, not wrinkled or shriveled. Stored in

the refrigerator in a plastic bag with a small piece of paper toweling tucked in to prevent moisture from collecting, it will keep for weeks. Fresh ginger is widely available and there is no suitable substitute.

Green onions (also called scallions): a primary seasoning in Chinese cooking. The whitish bulb portion is used in most dishes. The dark green upper stalks are included in stocks and some marinades and uncooked dishes, but are primarily reserved for use as garnish.

Hoisin sauce (also called seasoning sauce): a thick, dark brown, slightly sweet sauce made from soybeans, flour, sugar, garlic and spices. Available in cans and jars. Will keep indefinitely in tightly covered jar in refrigerator; if sauce begins to dry out, stir in a small amount of peanut oil. Sweet brown bean sauce, a similar product, can be substituted.

Mushrooms, dried black Chinese: have a strong, earthy flavor and vary in color from grayish-brown to almost black. Sizes include small (1 inch), medium (2 inch), large (3 inch) and extra-large (4 inch). The caps may be flat and fairly smooth or thick, round and deeply wrinkled. They must be softened and cleaned before using. After soaking they have a firm, slightly resistant but velvety texture. Used in Chinese cooking to provide flavor and texture. The soaking liquid is sometimes strained and used in the cooked dish to provide deeper flavor. Available loose or packaged; will keep indefinitely in covered container at room temperature. Dried Japanese shiitake mushrooms can be substituted for the Chinese dried mushrooms; but do not substitute fresh mushrooms or dried European mushrooms.

Mushrooms, golden: delicate, mild-flavored, creamy-yellow colored mushrooms with very long thin stems and tiny round caps. Available canned in salted water; also in jars under the Japanese name of nametake.

Mushrooms, straw: have squat yellowish-tan stems and pointed dark brown caps. They range in size from $\frac{3}{4}$ to $1\frac{3}{4}$ inches and have a mild delicate flavor and slippery silky texture. They are used in a variety of dishes, including soups and stir-frys. Available canned; drain and rinse before using.

Mustard green, pickled (also called salted mustard green): a Chinese vegetable with thick green stalks and thinner, darker green leaves. The flavor is similar to cabbage with a slight bitter aftertaste. Available in cans and jars and refrigerated in sealed plastic pouches; rinse well or soak in cold water to remove excess salt before using. Pickled mustard green can also be found in Japanese markets where it is called takana. If necessary, any Chinese pickled vegetable or Western sauerkraut can be substituted.

Napa: a member of the Chinese cabbage family, shorter and wider than celery cabbage. The head is oval-shaped and comprised primarily of full, tender, wrinkled leaves with a smaller proportion of crisp stalk. The color of the leaves ranges from almost pure white to medium-dark green. Uses and storage are the same as for celery cabbage.

Noodles, dried Chinese egg: thin straight noodles made of egg, wheat flour, water and salt. Can be simmered in soups, stir-fried with meat, fish or vegetables, or shallow-fried until crisp and golden and used as a bed for saucy stir-fried dishes. Available in 1 pound packages. Will keep indefinitely in tightly covered container in cool, dry place. Italian thin spaghetti, spaghettini or vermicelli can be substituted.

Noodles, rice stick (also called rice sticks or rice vermicelli): thin, slightly wavy, dried noodles made from rice flour. They are off-white in color, opaque and brittle. For use in soups and stir-frys, the noodles are first soaked briefly in warm water until softened before cooking. Available coiled in loose flat skeins in packages of various sizes. Will keep indefinitely in tightly covered container in cool dry place.

Oil, chili (also called chili pepper oil or hot pepper oil): reddish colored and fiery hot; flavoring oil made from peanut oil infused with dried red chili peppers. Use sparingly and according to personal taste. Available in small bottles; will keep indefinitely stored in cool dark place.

Oil, peanut: a pale golden colored cooking oil pressed from peanuts. It has a mild flavor and high smoking point which makes it ideal for stir-frying. Since peanut oil is much more expensive than other cooking oils, we recommend a good quality vegetable oil for deep-frying. Peanut oil is available in bottles and large cans.

Oil, sesame: a thick, dark brown, highly aromatic flavoring oil made from toasted sesame seeds. It has a rich nutty flavor and is used in small amounts. Sesame oil smokes and burns easily and therefore is not used as a cooking oil, but is added to a variety of dishes for flavor, sheen and aroma. Available in bottles and cans. Will keep for several months in a cool dark place. No substitute.

Oil, sesame chili (also called rayu): a reddish-brown flavoring oil added to dishes when both nutty and hot flavors are desired. Available in small glass bottles; will keep indefinitely stored in cool dark place.

Oyster sauce: a thick brown liquid of pourable consistency, made from oysters, salt, soy sauce and other seasonings. Flavor is rich and concentrated, with very little fish flavor. Used primarily in Cantonese-style dishes to impart color, body and flavor to sauces. Available in bottles and cans. Will keep indefinitely in tightly covered glass container in refrigerator.

Radish, pickled: the Chinese turnip or Japanese daikon which has been pickled with salt and sugar and sometimes other flavorings such as soy sauce or chili peppers. It is bright yellow or orange in color and is used to add a salty-sour flavor to a variety of dishes. Pickled radish is available in long sticks, slices and shredded; it is packed in cans, jars or sealed plastic pouches. In Japanese markets it is called takuan. It will keep refrigerated in its brine in tightly covered glass container for several weeks.

Rice, sweet (glutinous): small, oval-shaped, opaque-white rice grains which become very sticky and translucent when cooked. Used as a coating for steamed meat balls, in fillings and in desserts. Sweet rice is coated with starch and must be thoroughly rinsed and soaked before cooking. Sold by weight or in plastic bags. Store covered at room temperature.

Scallops, dried: scallops dehydrated into hard amber-colored discs, ½ to 1 inch in diameter. They have a concentrated flavor that cannot be duplicated by fresh scallops. Expensive and considered to be a delicacy, dried scallops are softened slightly in water, crumbled into shreds and used in small amounts in soups, stews and vegetable dishes. Sold by weight; will keep indefinitely tightly sealed in cool, dry place.

Sesame paste: a thick dark brown paste made from toasted sesame seeds with a strong rich nutty flavor and aroma. Available in jars; will keep covered with a thin layer of oil in refrigerator indefinitely. Middle Eastern tahini is equivalent to Oriental sesame paste. If necessary, peanut butter thinned with a little sesame oil can be substituted.

Shrimp, dried: small, salted, dehydrated shrimp, bright orange and very pungent in flavor. Dried shrimp are soaked in water to soften and remove excess salt; used sparingly in soups, stews and stir-frys to add flavor and a chewy texture. Sold prepackaged by weight; will keep indefinitely tightly sealed in cool, dry place. If necessary, Japanese dried shrimp can be substituted although they are smaller and less meaty, comprised mostly of shell.

Snow peas (also called Chinese pea pods): flat, bright green, fully edible pea pods harvested before the peas mature. Used in stir-frys for color, crunch and refreshing sweet flavor. Available fresh and frozen. Pinch off the tips of fresh snow peas and slowly pull them backward to remove the tough top string. Thaw frozen snow peas and drain thoroughly before using.

Soy sauce: a pungent, brown, salty liquid made of fermented soybeans, wheat, yeast, salt and sometimes sugar. It is an essential ingredient in Chinese cooking as a seasoning, flavor enhancer for other foods and a coloring. There are several grades of Chinese soy sauce (light, medium, and heavy) as well as Japanese-style soy sauce. Japanese soy sauce falls within the medium range. It is the kind most commonly available in the United States and has been used in testing the recipes in this book.

Star anise: a dry, brown spice in the shape of an 8-pointed star; each point of the star contains a shiny round seed. Used primarily in simmered dishes where it imparts a distinct licorice flavor and aroma. Sold by weight. Stored tightly covered in cool dark place it will retain its potency for a year or longer.

Szechuan peppercorns (also called fagara): reddish-brown, open-husked peppercorns with distinct pungent aroma. They have a mildly hot flavor and produce a slight tingling sensation in the mouth. Sold by weight or in small packages. Will keep indefinitely stored in tightly sealed jar in cool dark place.

Turnip, Chinese (also called white or icicle turnip): a white root vegetable, 8 to 12 inches long and 3 to 4 inches in diameter, with crisp light texture similar to the Western radish but with a stronger flavor and a peppery bite. Will keep in refrigerator tightly wrapped in plastic up to 2 weeks. The Japanese daikon (icicle radish) can be substituted.

Vinegar, Chinese black (also called Chenkong rice vinegar): an aged rice vinegar, very dark brown in color with a strong but mellow flavor. Available in bottles; will keep indefinitely in cool dark place. The flavor is unique, but if necessary, a mild red wine vinegar can be substituted.

Vinegar, rice (also called white rice vinegar): ranges in color from almost white to pale gold; mellow and mildly tangy in flavor. Avoid brands that are seasoned with salt or sugar. Available in bottles; will keep indefinitely in cool dark place.

Water chestnuts: walnut-sized bulbs from an aquatic plant. The bulb has a tough brown skin and crisp white interior. Used to add crunchy texture and mild flavor to stir-fried dishes and fillings. Fresh water chestnuts are superior to canned but are not so widely available.

Wine, rice: a staple ingredient in Chinese cooking, it can be clear white but generally has a pale to deep gold color. Choose one that is rich and mellow in flavor, with no harsh or bitter undertones. Avoid products labeled Chinese cooking wine, as they have salt or sugar added and are of inferior quality. Do not use sake, the Japanese rice wine, or mirin, a sweetened Japanese cooking wine. If you cannot find a good quality Chinese rice wine, substitute a good quality dry sherry.

Wonton skins (also called gyoza or dumpling skins): similar to egg roll wrappers, these skins are available in 3 to 3½-inch squares or circles. Available fresh or frozen. See egg roll wrappers for buying and storing information.

Dim Sum

Crisp-Fried Crescents

3 medium dried black
   Chinese mushrooms
1 teaspoon cornstarch
1 teaspoon cold water
2 teaspoons soy sauce
2 teaspoons rice wine
2 tablespoons peanut oil
½ pound ground pork or
   beef, march-chopped
½ cup finely chopped yellow
   onion
½ cup finely chopped canned
   water chestnuts
1 to 2 teaspoons curry powder
½ teaspoon sugar
30 to 36 round wonton skins
1 small egg, lightly beaten
4 cups vegetable oil

Variation: Substitute 1½ cups canned sweetened red bean paste for meat filling. Fill and seal as in Step 3. Dip end of wooden chopstick into red food coloring and "dot" each crescent to indicate sweet filling. Fry as in Step 4. Serve between courses of meal to refresh palate or as a snack or dessert.

1. Soften and clean mushrooms; mince. Mix cornstarch and cold water in a cup until smooth; stir in soy sauce and rice wine.

2. Heat wok over high heat 15 seconds; add peanut oil and heat until hot, about 30 seconds. Add meat; stir-fry, breaking meat up into fine pieces, until light brown, 2½

to 3 minutes. Add onion; stir-fry until translucent, 45 seconds. Add water chestnuts and mushrooms; stir-fry 45 seconds. Add curry powder; stir-fry 20 seconds. Stir cornstarch mixture and add to wok; add sugar. Cook and stir until thickened, 30 seconds. Remove meat mixture with slotted spoon to bowl, draining well. Discard excess oil. Cool filling completely.

3. Spread 6 wonton skins in single layer on flat surface; brush top surface of each skin lightly with egg. Place a heaping teaspoon of filling in center of each skin. Fold skin in half to enclose filling and form crescent. Pinch edges

firmly together to seal. Press edges with tines of fork for decorative edge. Place filled crescents in single layer on tray or plate lined with clean cloth. Repeat until all filling has been used.

4. Heat wok over high heat 20 seconds; add vegetable oil and heat to 375°F. Fry ⅓ of crescents at a time, turning frequently, until golden, 2½ to 3½ minutes. Remove with strainer; drain on paper toweling. Keep warm in 200°F oven. Reheat oil to 375°F and repeat with remaining crescents. Serve immediately.
Makes 2½ to 3 dozen

Pearl Balls

½ cup sweet (glutinous) rice
2 to 3 drops yellow food coloring, if desired
3 large dried black Chinese mushrooms
½ pound ground pork or beef, march-chopped
1 small egg white, lightly beaten
1 tablespoon minced green onion, white part only
1½ teaspoons soy sauce
1½ teaspoons rice wine
½ teaspoon minced pared fresh ginger root
½ teaspoon sugar
¼ teaspoon salt
Pinch pepper
1½ teaspoons cornstarch
Boiling water

GARLIC-SOY SAUCE
3 tablespoons soy sauce
1½ tablespoons distilled white vinegar
¼ teaspoon minced garlic
⅛ teaspoon sugar

1. Place rice in medium bowl of cold water. Comb through rice with fingers several times;

drain. Repeat until water remains clear. Return rice to bowl; fill with warm tap water. Stir in food coloring. Soak rice 3 to 4 hours, or refrigerate, covered, overnight.

2. Soften and clean mushrooms; mince. Drain rice well. Spread in even layer on plate. Combine all ingredients except rice, cornstarch, boiling water and Garlic-Soy Sauce; mix well. Stir in cornstarch.

3. Shape meat mixture into 1-inch balls; mixture will be fairly soft. Roll each ball in the

rice to coat completely; press lightly between hands to make rice adhere.*

4. Place pearl balls in single layer in steamer basket lined

with wet cloth; leave about ½-inch space between balls; cover. Place steamer in wok; add boiling water to wok to level of 1 inch below steamer. Steam over high heat 40 minutes. Add boiling water as needed.

5. Mix ingredients for Garlic-Soy Sauce in small bowl.

6. Transfer pearl balls from steamer to serving dish. Spoon about ⅛ teaspoon Garlic-Soy Sauce over each ball or pass sauce separately for dipping.
Makes about 18 pearl balls

Pearl balls can be made through Step 3 up to 8 hours ahead; refrigerate, covered with plastic wrap; uncover and let stand at room temperature 15 to 20 minutes before steaming. Recipe can be doubled if you have 2 steamer baskets.

Sesame-Nut Chicken Sticks

12 large chicken wings
¾ teaspoon salt
⅛ teaspoon pepper
1 tablespoon rice wine
Sweet and Sour Dipping Sauce (see Index for page number)
Roasted Pepper-Salt (see Index for page number)
1 thin cucumber (for garnish)
1 large strawberry, hulled (for garnish)
4 tablespoons cornstarch
1 tablespoon cold water
2 large egg yolks
2 tablespoons all-purpose flour
½ cup white sesame seeds
½ cup finely chopped peanuts, cashews or almonds
5 cups vegetable oil
3 large fresh parsley sprigs, if desired

1. Detach first joints and wing tips. (Retain for other use.) Prepare remaining middle joints: Cut through skin and meat around one end of wing;

cut tendons to detach meat from end of bone. Stand wing upright; push skin and meat downward. Insert knife between the two exposed bones; cut between bones to disconnect them.

2. Grasp the smaller bone; twist and pull to detach it from meaty end. Discard small bone. Pull chicken meat and skin as far down as possible; flatten. Place chicken wings in single layer; sprinkle with ½ teaspoon salt and the pepper. Drizzle with rice wine; rub over meat to coat

evenly. Reserve at room temperature 30 minutes.

3. Meanwhile, make Sweet and Sour Dipping Sauce and Roasted Pepper-Salt.

4. For garnish: Slant-cut cucumber at ⅛-inch intervals, leaving slices attached ⅜-inch from bottom on first 7 cuts; detach piece on eighth cut. Cut a V-shaped wedge from center of each cucumber piece; do not detach slices. Cut strawberry into 6 wedges; place 1 wedge in center of each cucumber piece. Refrigerate.

5. Mix 1 tablespoon cornstarch and the cold water until smooth; whisk in egg yolks until smooth. Stir in flour and ¼ teaspoon salt to form smooth thick batter. Spread sesame seeds and peanuts on separate plates; dust a third plate with 1 tablespoon cornstarch.

6. Pat chicken wings dry with paper toweling. Coat ½ of chicken, one piece at a time: Dip into 2 tablespoons cornstarch; brush off excess. Dip into batter; shake off excess. Dip into sesame seeds to coat both sides; press firmly between palms. Place on cornstarch-coated plate. Repeat with remaining chicken, dipping into peanuts to coat.

7. Heat wok over high heat 20 seconds; add oil and heat to 325°F. Reduce heat to medium. Add chicken to wok. Fry, turning occasionally, 3 minutes. Increase heat to high; fry until coating is light brown and crisp and chicken is cooked, 3 to 4 minutes. Drain on paper toweling.

8. Arrange chicken wings on serving platter with cucumber garnish and parsley. Serve with Sweet and Sour Dipping Sauce and Roasted Pepper-Salt.
Makes 12 pieces

Pork and Crab Egg Rolls

4 ounces boneless pork
   shoulder
2 tablespoons rice wine
3 teaspoons cornstarch
2 ounces canned bamboo
   shoots, rinsed and drained
½ small green bell pepper
2 ounces fresh or thawed
   frozen crab meat
3 medium dried black
   Chinese mushrooms,
   softened and cleaned
1 tablespoon soy sauce
2 tablespoons lard
2 tablespoons minced green
   onion, white part only
1 teaspoon minced pared
   fresh ginger root
1 cup finely shredded celery
   cabbage
1 teaspoon sesame oil, if
   desired
8 Egg Roll Wrappers (recipe
   follows)
1 small egg, beaten
6 cups vegetable oil
Romaine lettuce leaves

If desired, square commercial egg roll wrappers can be used. Omit Step 5 and fill as follows: Place wrapper with one point toward you. Place filling in a row about 3 inches long midway between the point nearest you and the center. Brush all edges of wrapper with beaten egg. Fold point nearest you over filling to enclose; brush newly exposed edges with egg. Fold sides of wrapper over filling; firmly roll up egg roll, pressing edge to seal.

1. Cut pork across the grain into ⅛-inch thick slices; stack slices and cut lengthwise into ⅛-inch wide shreds. Combine pork, 1 tablespoon rice wine and 2 teaspoons cornstarch in small bowl; stir to mix well. Marinate at room temperature 30 minutes.

2. Cut bamboo shoots into 2 × 1/16 × 1/16-inch pieces. Cut green pepper into 1/16-inch wide shreds; cut shreds into 2-inch lengths. Break crab meat into fine shreds with fingers, picking out any bits of shell or cartilage. Cut mushrooms into 1/16-inch wide shreds.

3. Mix 1 teaspoon cornstarch and 1 tablespoon rice wine in a cup until smooth; stir in soy sauce.

4. Heat wok over high heat 15 seconds; add lard and heat until melted and hot, about 30 seconds. Scatter in pork; stir-fry 1 minute. Add onion and ginger; stir-fry 10 seconds. Add bamboo shoots, mushrooms, cabbage, green pepper and crab, separately and in order; stir-fry 15 seconds after each addition. Stir cornstarch mixture and add to wok; cook and stir 1 minute. Stir in sesame oil; transfer filling to plate. Cool completely, uncovered.

5. Place one Egg Roll Wrapper, golden-side-up, with cut edge toward you. Spread 2½ tablespoons filling in a row about 4 inches long along the cut edge.

6. Fold the two sides of wrapper over filling. Brush side pieces and rounded edge of wrapper with beaten egg. Neatly and firmly roll up egg roll; press edge to seal. Repeat to fill 8 egg rolls.

7. Heat wok over high heat 20 seconds; add vegetable oil and heat to 375°F. Carefully add egg rolls to wok. Fry, turning occasionally, until egg rolls are golden and crisp, 3½ to 4 minutes. Remove rolls with strainer; drain on paper toweling. Arrange on plate lined with lettuce leaves. Serve immediately.

Makes 8 egg rolls

Egg Roll Wrappers

1 small egg
¾ cup cold water
¼ teaspoon salt
¾ cup plus 2 tablespoons
  all-purpose flour
2 tablespoons peanut oil

1. Beat egg in medium bowl; whisk in water and salt. Add flour, ⅓ at a time, whisking until smooth after each addition. Reserve at room temperature 15 minutes.*

2. Heat wok over high heat 15 seconds; add 1 tablespoon oil and heat until hot, about 15 seconds. Turn off heat; wipe inside of wok with paper toweling; leave thin coating of oil.

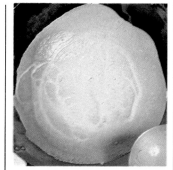

3. Heat wok over low heat 15 seconds. Leave heat on but remove wok from heat. Stir batter; pour ¼ cup around side of wok in an 8-inch circle. Quickly rotate wok to fill in the circle with an even layer of batter; return wok to heat. Fill in any tiny holes that form by

brushing with small amount of batter. (If batter sets before you can fill the circle by rotating or if too many holes form, wok is too hot. If batter does not set quickly enough, leaving edges of circle paper-thin, wok is not hot enough. Adjust heat accordingly.)

4. Cook wrapper until batter is set, bottom is slightly golden and edges begin to pull away from wok, 45 seconds to 1 minute. Carefully grasp one edge of wrapper with fingertips; quickly and carefully lift and peel it off. Gently place wrapper flat on paper toweling, golden-side-down.

5. Repeat Steps 2, 3 and 4 using low heat throughout and using 1 teaspoon oil for each wrapper, to make a total of 4 circles. Cool completely. Cut each wrapper in half to yield 8 half-circle wrappers.

*Homemade egg roll wrappers are more tender and delicate than the commercial variety. If making homemade wrappers for the first time, you might make a double batch of batter to allow for some mistakes as you learn the technique.

Double-Fried Pork Strips

Roasted Pepper-Salt (see Index for page number)
Sweet and Sour Dipping Sauce (see Index for page number) or hoisin sauce
1 pound pork tenderloin
1 tablespoon rice wine
1 tablespoon soy sauce
¾ teaspoon salt
½ teaspoon sugar
⅛ teaspoon pepper
1 tomato (for garnish)
6 Romaine lettuce leaves
½ cup plus 2 tablespoons cornstarch
1 cup cold water
1 large egg
1⅓ cups all-purpose flour
1 tablespoon baking powder
2 tablespoons peanut oil
4 cups vegetable oil
1½ tablespoons minced fresh coriander

1. Prepare Roasted Pepper-Salt and Sweet and Sour Dipping Sauce.

2. Cut pork lengthwise, with the grain, into ½-inch thick slices; cut slices across the

grain into 2×½-inch strips. Mix rice wine, soy sauce, ¼ teaspoon salt, the sugar and pepper in medium bowl; stir in pork strips. Marinate at room temperature 30 minutes.

3. For garnish: Cut tomato into 6 wedges. With paring knife, cut skin and very thin layer of tomato flesh from each wedge, leaving it attached at base. Fold skin back to form petal. Arrange lettuce leaves and tomato garnish on serving dish; refrigerate covered.

4. Mix ½ cup cornstarch in the cold water in small bowl until smooth; whisk into egg in medium bowl. Whisk in flour and ½ teaspoon salt until smooth. Whisk baking powder into batter; let stand until bubbly, about 5 minutes. Stir in peanut oil.

5. Heat wok over high heat 20 seconds; add vegetable oil and heat to 375°F. Pat pork strips dry with paper toweling. Shake in bag with 2 tablespoons cornstarch to coat evenly; shake off excess.

6. Fry ½ of pork strips as follows: Dip each pork strip into batter; add to wok. (Batter should thickly coat pork; if it seems too thick, stir in 1 to 2 tablespoons additional water.) Fry 8 pork strips at a time, stirring gently, until golden, 3 to 4 minutes. Remove with strainer and drain on paper toweling. When ½ of pork is fried, stir coriander into re-

maining batter. Reheat oil to 375°F; dip and fry remaining pork as above.

7. Heat oil to 375°F. Fry pork again, ½ at a time (do not dip in batter again), until crisp and light brown, 3 to 4 minutes. Remove with strainer and drain on wire rack lined with paper toweling.

8. Arrange pork on prepared serving dish. Serve immediately with Roasted Pepper-Salt and Sweet and Sour Dipping Sauce.
Makes 4 to 6 servings

Steamed Chinese Bread

1 teaspoon active dry yeast
½ cup plus 1 tablespoon very warm water (105°F to 115°F)
1 tablespoon sugar
2⅓ to 2⅔ cups all-purpose flour
1 tablespoon lard
½ teaspoon peanut or sesame oil
Lard
½ teaspoon baking powder
Boiling water

1. Dissolve yeast in 1 tablespoon water in small bowl. Stir in ½ cup water and the sugar; let stand until bubbly, 10 minutes.

2. Combine 2 cups flour and 1 tablespoon lard in medium bowl. Rub lard into flour with fingers until mixture has fine even texture.

3. Make depression in center of flour mixture; add yeast

mixture. Stir to form stiff dough. Knead on lightly floured surface, using remaining flour as needed to prevent sticking, until smooth and elastic, 5 to 10 minutes.

4. Oil a clean medium bowl. Place dough in bowl; turn over. Let rise, covered, in warm draft-free place until doubled, about 1 hour.

5. Cut eight pieces of parchment or waxed paper, 3½×2 inches. Lightly grease one side of each piece with lard.

6. Turn dough out onto lightly floured surface; pat into ¾-inch thick rectangle. Sprinkle evenly with baking powder; fold in thirds. Knead, using remaining flour as needed to prevent sticking, until very stiff, smooth and elastic, about 5 minutes.

7. Roll dough into a smooth log, 8 inches long. Cut cross-

wise into 1-inch wide pieces; dip knife in flour to prevent sticking. Place on greased piece of paper. Place in steamer basket lined with wet cloth, spacing evenly. Let rise, covered, until doubled, 30 to 45 minutes.

8. Cover steamer; place in wok. Add boiling water to wok to level of 1 inch below steamer. Steam, covered, over high heat 15 minutes. Remove steamer from wok. Wait 10 seconds; uncover. Serve warm or at room temperature.
Makes 8 pieces

Rice-Filled Shao Mai

¾ cup sweet (glutinous) rice
¾ cup water
2 ounces skinless, boneless chicken breast
2 ounces ham
1½ ounces canned bamboo shoots, rinsed and drained
2 medium dried black Chinese mushrooms, softened and cleaned
¼ cup chicken stock or broth
3 tablespoons soy sauce
2 tablespoons rice wine
1½ teaspoons sugar
⅛ teaspoon pepper
3 tablespoons lard
2 tablespoons minced green onion, white part only
2 teaspoons minced pared fresh ginger root
24 to 28 round wonton skins
Cornstarch
3 tablespoons peas (for garnish)
Boiling water

1. Place rice in medium bowl of cold water. Comb through with fingers several times; drain. Repeat until water remains clear. Return rice to bowl; fill with warm tap water. Soak at room temperature 1 hour.

2. Drain rice; combine with ¾ cup water in small saucepan. Heat to boiling; reduce heat to low. Cook, covered, 5 minutes. Remove from heat; let stand, covered, 10 minutes. Transfer rice to medium bowl; cool completely, uncovered.

3. Dice chicken into ¼-inch cubes. Dice ham, bamboo shoots and mushrooms into 3/16-inch cubes. Mix stock, soy sauce, rice wine, sugar and pepper in small bowl.

4. Heat wok over high heat 15 seconds; add lard and heat until melted and hot, about 30 seconds. Add chicken to wok; stir-fry 30 seconds. Add bamboo shoots and mushrooms; stir-fry 30 seconds. Stir in stock mixture; heat to boiling. Add ham, onion and ginger; cook and stir 30 seconds. Transfer to plate; cool, uncovered, 15 minutes. Add to rice; stir to mix well.

5. Dust 2 wonton skins lightly with cornstarch; stack the 2 skins and roll to 4-inch diameter. Lay one skin in palm of hand. Place 1½ tablespoons filling in center, spreading slightly.

6. Cup palm to bring edges of skin up around filling; skin will begin to fold and pleat. Squeeze firmly from below, while pressing filling from above with spatula to make filling adhere.

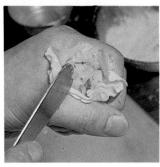

7. Hold shao mai with thumb and index finger encircling upper portion. Continue squeezing until filling is ¼-inch from top; squeeze with thumb and index finger to form slight indentation while twisting a half turn. Flatten bottom slightly so it will stand upright. Repeat until all filling is used. Top each shao mai with one pea.

8. Place heatproof plate in steamer basket; arrange shao mai on plate in single layer ½ inch apart. Cover steamer with damp cloth and lid.

9. Place steamer in wok; add boiling water to wok to level of 1 inch below steamer. Steam, covered, over medium heat 20 minutes. If using more than one steamer, reverse positions after first 10 minutes of steaming. Check water level; add boiling water as needed. Serve immediately.

Makes 24 to 30

Spinach Shao Mai

8 ounces fresh spinach, cleaned and stemmed
4 ounces fresh white mushrooms, minced
6 ounces ground pork, march-chopped
2 tablespoons minced green onion, white part only
2 teaspoons minced pared fresh ginger root
2 teaspoons rice wine
1 teaspoon soy sauce
½ teaspoon salt
⅛ teaspoon pepper
20 to 24 wonton skins, 3-inch square
Boiling water

1. Cook spinach with water that clings to leaves, covered, in wok over medium-high heat, stirring occasionally, until slightly wilted, 1 minute. Remove spinach; cool.

2. Squeeze spinach to remove excess moisture; chop finely. Combine all ingredients, except skins and water; stir to mix thoroughly.

3. Lay a wonton skin on outstretched fingers of one hand. Place about 1 tablespoon filling in center, spreading slightly. Gather edges of skin upward around filling; skin will begin to fold and pleat. Push folds lightly into filling with spatula; begin to form elongated shape.

4. Hold shao mai with thumb and index finger encircling upper portion. Squeeze gently to narrow and lengthen; push down on filling with spatula while squeezing to prevent overflow.

5. Squeeze near top of shao mai with thumb and index finger to form slight indentation. Flatten bottom slightly so it will stand upright. Repeat until all filling is used.

6. Steam and serve following directions in Steps 8 and 9 of "Rice-Filled Shao Mai" (recipe above).

Makes 20 to 24

Soups

Chinese Bean Curd Soup

½ ounce dried shrimp
½ cup boiling water
14 ounces bean curd
1 can (10 ounces) golden
    mushrooms, rinsed and
    drained
3 ounces canned bamboo
    shoots, rinsed and drained
1½ tablespoons cornstarch
3 tablespoons cold water
2 teaspoons peanut oil
1 large egg, at room
    temperature
⅛ ounce dried cloud ears,
    softened and cleaned
4 cups chicken stock or broth
2 tablespoons rice wine
¾ teaspoon salt
⅛ teaspoon white pepper

1. Rinse shrimp under warm running water, rubbing between fingers. Place shrimp in small bowl; add boiling water. Soak at room temperature 1 hour.

2. Cut bean curd into ½-inch cubes; drain on several layers of paper toweling. Arrange mushrooms in elongated pile; cut crosswise through pile at ¾-inch intervals. Cut bamboo shoots lengthwise into ¹⁄₁₆-inch thick slices. Stack several slices at a time and cut into ¾-inch pieces.

3. Mix cornstarch and cold water in a cup until smooth; stir in 1 teaspoon oil. Beat egg in small bowl just until yolk and white are thoroughly combined; stir in 1 teaspoon oil.

4. Remove shrimp from soaking liquid; reserve liquid. Mince shrimp. Break cloud ears into ½-inch pieces.

5. Combine chicken stock, bamboo shoots, shrimp and reserved soaking liquid in wok; heat over high heat to boiling. Reduce heat to maintain simmer; simmer, uncovered, 5 minutes. Add bean curd, cloud ears, rice wine, salt and pepper to wok; heat over high heat to boiling. Reduce heat; simmer, uncovered 3 minutes. Stir in mushrooms; cook 30 seconds.

6. Reduce heat to very low. Stir cornstarch mixture; slowly pour into wok, stirring constantly. Cook and stir until soup is slightly thickened, about 1 minute.

7. Turn off heat. Gently pour egg into soup in wide circle; let stand undisturbed 15 seconds. Gently stir 2 or 3 times. Pour soup into heated serving bowl. Serve immediately.
Makes 4 to 6 servings

Variation: For hot and sour soup, mix 2 tablespoons Chinese black vinegar, 1 tablespoon soy sauce and ½ teaspoon chili oil in serving bowl; add soup, stir and serve.

Soup of Sole and Vegetables

4 ounces pickled mustard green, rinsed and drained
4 ounces canned whole bamboo shoots, rinsed and drained
2 ounces fresh spinach, cleaned
1 small egg white
2 tablespoons plus 2 teaspoons rice wine
¾ to 1¼ teaspoons salt
⅛ teaspoon plus pinch white pepper
3 tablespoons cornstarch
¾ pound skinless sole or flounder fillets
6 cups chicken stock or broth
2 tablespoons finely chopped green onion, white part only
1 teaspoon minced pared fresh ginger root
1 tablespoon rice vinegar

1. Spread mustard green flat on board. Hold knife at about 20° angle to board and shave off paper-thin slices of mustard green, less than ¹⁄₁₆-inch thick.

2. Cut bamboo shoots lengthwise into ¹⁄₁₆-inch thick slices. Remove spinach stems; stack leaves and cut crosswise into ¼-inch wide strips.

3. Combine egg white, 2 teaspoons rice wine, ¼ teaspoon salt and the pinch of pepper in shallow bowl; whisk lightly to combine. Spread cornstarch on plate.

4. Cut fish into 3×2-inch pieces. Dip fish pieces, one at a time, into egg white mixture to coat both sides; drain off excess. Dip fish in cornstarch to coat both sides lightly; shake off excess. Place fish in single layer on a second plate.

5. Combine chicken stock, mustard green, bamboo shoots, 2 tablespoons rice wine, the onion and ginger in wok. Heat over high heat to boiling; reduce heat to medium. Cook uncovered 5 minutes.

6. Slip fish pieces, one at a time, into wok. Add spinach; stir gently once or twice. Cook, uncovered, just until fish turns white and is cooked through, 1 to 1½ minutes. Stir in vinegar, ½ to 1 teaspoon salt and ⅛ teaspoon pepper. Serve immediately.

Makes 4 servings

Chicken and Vegetables with Noodles

2 pounds chicken legs and thighs
¾ pound fresh Chinese turnip, pared
¾ pound carrots, pared
4 green onions, white part only
4 thin slices fresh ginger root
5 quarts plus 5 cups water
⅓ cup rice wine
2½ teaspoons salt
⅛ teaspoon pepper
½ pound dried Chinese egg noodles
1 tablespoon peanut oil

1. Cut chicken pieces crosswise into about 1-inch wide pieces. Use a cleaver or chef's knife and a meat mallet or hammer if needed to pound cleaver through bones.

2. Cut turnip into 1-inch cubes. If desired, cut off corners of each cube at an angle, making multi-faceted balls. Roll-cut carrots into 1¼-inch

pieces. Cut onions into 1-inch lengths. Pare ginger root. Pound green onions and ginger lightly with flat side of cleaver.

3. Heat 2 quarts water in wok to boiling. Add chicken pieces; stir. Cook 1 minute after water returns to boiling. Quickly remove chicken with slotted spoon to sieve (do not turn off heat); rinse under cold running water to cool. Transfer to bowl. Add carrots to boiling water in wok; cook 1 minute after water returns to boiling. Remove carrots with slotted spoon to sieve; rinse

under cold running water to cool. Transfer carrots to second bowl. Repeat process with turnips, adding them to carrots in second bowl.

4. Combine 5 cups water, the rice wine, onions and ginger in wok; heat over high heat to boiling. Add chicken; when water returns to boiling, reduce heat to low. Skim foam from surface. Simmer chicken, covered, 20 minutes.

5. Add turnip and carrots to wok; stir. Simmer, covered, until vegetables are tender, about 20 minutes longer. Stir

in 1½ teaspoons salt and the pepper. Keep soup hot.

6. Heat 3 quarts water and 1 teaspoon salt in large pot to boiling. Add noodles; cook until firm-tender, 3 to 6 minutes after water returns to boiling. Drain noodles; rinse briefly under hot running water and drain well. Drizzle noodles with oil; toss to coat. Divide noodles among individual serving bowls. Ladle soup over noodles. Serve immediately.

Makes 4 to 6 servings

Bean Sprout Soup

¾ pound fresh soy bean
   sprouts
4 green onions, white part
   only
½ pound ground pork,
   march-chopped
1½ teaspoons minced pared
   fresh ginger root
1 small egg, lightly beaten
3½ tablespoons rice wine
1 tablespoon water
½ teaspoon salt
Pinch pepper
2 tablespoons cornstarch
1 tablespoon peanut oil
4 cups chicken stock or broth
1 tablespoon soy sauce

1. Pinch off and discard hairy tips of bean sprouts. Rinse sprouts and drain well. Mince 1 onion. Cut remaining 3 onions diagonally into ½-inch lengths.

2. Combine pork, minced onion and ½ teaspoon ginger in medium bowl. Add egg, 1½ tablespoons rice wine, the water, salt and pepper. Mix firmly and thoroughly with hand until mixture is smooth. Add cornstarch; stir to mix well. Spread oil on a 6- to 7-inch plate, including rim.

Shape pork mixture into smooth even patty, about 6 inches in diameter, on oiled plate.

3. Heat wok over high heat 15 seconds; add 2 cups stock and remaining onions, 2 tablespoons rice wine and 1 teaspoon ginger. Add sprouts to wok; spread in even layer.

Slide pork patty into center of wok. Heat to boiling; reduce heat to low. Simmer, covered, until sprouts are tender, 12 to 15 minutes.

4. Add 2 cups stock to wok; heat to boiling. Stir in soy sauce. Transfer soup to heated serving bowl. To serve, cut pork patty into 4 even wedges and serve with sprouts and stock. Serve immediately.
   Makes 4 servings

Rice Noodle Soup

3 chicken thighs (about 12
   ounces) or 8 ounces
   boneless chicken breast
3 ounces canned bamboo
   shoots, rinsed and drained
2 ounces sliced ham
2 ounces chicken giblets,
   rinsed and drained, if
   desired
4 leaves napa or celery
   cabbage
4 small dried black Chinese
   mushrooms, softened and
   cleaned
6 ounces rice stick noodles
5 tablespoons peanut oil
8 medium shrimp, shelled
   and deveined
6 cups chicken stock or broth
2 tablespoons rice wine
1 teaspoon salt
3 tablespoons soy sauce
⅛ teaspoon pepper

1. Bone chicken thighs following directions in Steps 2 and 3 of "Chicken Stir-Fry with Radish" (see Index for page number). Cut chicken into 1½×1-inch pieces. Cut bamboo shoots lengthwise into ¼-inch thick slices; cut

slices crosswise into 1½-inch pieces. Cut ham into 1-inch pieces. Cut chicken gizzard and liver into 1-inch pieces. Cut cabbage into 1-inch pieces. Slant-cut mushrooms into 3 pieces each.

2. Soak rice sticks in large bowl of warm tap water 5 minutes. Drain well.

3. Heat wok over high heat 15 seconds; add oil and heat until hot, about 30 seconds. Add chicken; stir-fry until no longer pink, about 2 minutes. Add bamboo shoots and mushrooms; stir-fry 30 seconds. Add giblets; stir-fry 15

seconds. Add ham, shrimp and cabbage; stir-fry 1 minute.

4. Add stock, rice wine and salt to wok; heat to boiling. Reduce heat to medium; skim foam. Cook soup, uncovered, 5 minutes. Add rice sticks to

one side of wok; do not stir. Cook, uncovered, until noodles are tender, 2 to 3 minutes.

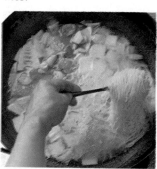

5. Remove as many noodles as possible with fork to center of serving bowl. Stir soy sauce and pepper into soup in wok; ladle soup around noodles in bowl. Serve immediately.
   Makes 6 to 8 servings

Chinese Pepper Steak

¾ pound boneless top sirloin
3 tablespoons soy sauce
3 tablespoons rice wine
1½ teaspoons sugar
1½ tablespoons cornstarch
6 tablespoons peanut oil
3 medium green bell peppers
1 can (10½ ounces) bamboo
 shoots, rinsed and drained
4 green onions, white part
 only
3 thin slices fresh ginger root
1 tablespoon sesame oil

1. To facilitate slicing, freeze beef until firm but not frozen, 20 to 30 minutes. Cut beef across the grain into ⅛-inch thick slices. Stack slices; cut into 1¼-inch squares.

2. Mix 1½ tablespoons each soy sauce and rice wine and 1 teaspoon sugar in medium bowl; stir in beef. Sprinkle with cornstarch; stir to mix well. Stir in 1 tablespoon peanut oil. Marinate at room temperature 30 minutes.

3. Cut green peppers diagonally into 1×1½-inch pieces. Cut bamboo shoots lengthwise into thin slices; cut slices into 1½-inch pieces. Cut onions into ½-inch pieces. Pare ginger root; cut into small squares.

4. Mix 1½ tablespoons each soy sauce and rice wine and ½ teaspoon sugar in small bowl.

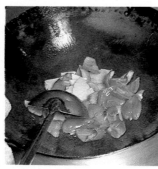

5. Heat wok over high heat 15 seconds; add 2 tablespoons peanut oil and heat until hot, about 30 seconds. Scatter in green peppers and bamboo shoots; stir-fry 2 minutes. Transfer to plate.

6. Add 3 tablespoons peanut oil to wok; heat until hot. Reduce heat to medium; stir-fry onions and ginger 10 seconds. Increase heat to high and scatter in beef, ¼ at a time; stir-fry 1 minute after all beef is added. Return green peppers and bamboo shoots to wok;

stir-fry 30 seconds. Stir in soy sauce mixture; cook and stir until meat and vegetables are coated with sauce, 30 to 45 seconds. Drizzle with sesame oil; stir 3 or 4 times. Serve immediately.
Makes 3 to 4 servings

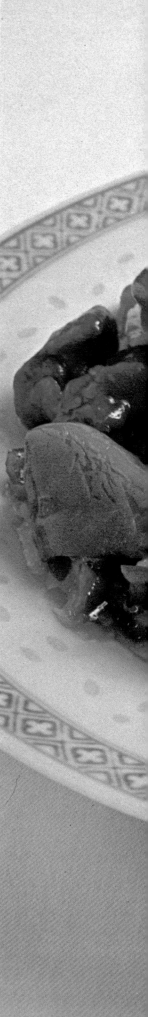

Five-Spice Steamed Pork

8 thin slices fresh ginger root
4 green onions, white part
　　only
1 clove garlic
1½ pounds boneless pork
　　loin blade (rib end)
Boiling water
5 tablespoons soy sauce
4 cups vegetable oil
1 cup chicken stock or broth
1 tablespoon rice wine
1 tablespoon sugar
¼ teaspoon five-spice
　　powder
1½ pounds fresh spinach,
　　cleaned
3 tablespoons peanut oil
1 tablespoon cornstarch
1½ tablespoons cold water

1. Pare ginger root. Lightly pound ginger, onions and garlic with flat side of cleaver.

2. Rinse pork; place fat-side-down in wok. Add boiling water to cover. Heat over high heat to boiling; boil 2 minutes. Adjust heat to maintain strong

simmer, medium-low. Skim foam; add 6 ginger slices and 2 onions. Cook, covered, until juices run clear when pork is pierced to center with knife, 45 minutes; turn pork after 25 minutes. Drain; discard liquid. Wipe wok clean.

3. Place pork in bowl that will hold it snugly. Add 2 table-spoons soy sauce; rub into pork on all sides. Marinate, turning occasionally, 30 minutes.

4. Heat wok over high heat 20 seconds; add vegetable oil and heat to 350°F. Drain pork; pat dry with paper toweling. Add pork to wok; reduce heat to medium. Fry, turning once, until well browned, 2½ to 3 minutes per side. Remove pork; drain on paper toweling. Cool pork 15 minutes. Remove oil from wok; wipe clean.

5. Combine chicken stock, 3 tablespoons soy sauce, the rice wine, sugar and five-spice powder; stir until sugar dissolves.

6. Select a heatproof bowl just large enough to hold pork and stock mixture. Cut pork across the grain into ⅛-inch thick slices; stack slices in original shape. Place pork, fat-side-down in bowl. Add stock mixture, garlic, 2 ginger slices and 2 onions; liquid should just cover top of pork. Cover bowl with foil; place in steamer basket. Cover steamer; place in wok. Add boiling water to

wok to level of 1 inch below steamer. Steam over medium-high heat 1½ hours. Add boiling water as needed.

7. Trim spinach; leave 2 inches of stem attached. Pat dry with paper toweling.

8. Remove steamer from wok. Empty wok; wipe dry. Heat wok over high heat 15 seconds, add peanut oil and heat until hot, 30 seconds. Add spinach. (Oil may spatter when adding spinach.) Stir-fry until bright green, 1 minute. Arrange on platter. Remove pork slices from liquid; arrange overlapping on spinach. Discard ginger, onions and garlic.

9. Transfer liquid in bowl to wok. Heat over high heat to boiling. Mix cornstarch and cold water until smooth; add to wok. Cook and stir until thickened, 45 seconds. Pour over pork.

Makes 4 to 6 servings

Liver with Onions and Chili Peppers

1 pound sliced baby beef liver
3 tablespoons soy sauce
2 tablespoons rice wine
1 teaspoon sugar
1 tablespoon plus 1 teaspoon
　　cornstarch
2 teaspoons sesame oil
Boiling water
3 dried red chili peppers
⅛ ounce dried cloud ears,
　　softened and cleaned
10 green onions, white part
　　only
3 large stalks celery
2 tablespoons cold water
1 tablespoon rice vinegar
5 tablespoons peanut oil
2 teaspoons minced pared
　　fresh ginger root

1. Rinse liver; pat dry. Cut or pull off thin skin around edge of liver, discard. Cut out large

veins; discard. Cut liver into long shreds, ³⁄₁₆-inch wide.

2. Mix 2 tablespoons soy sauce, 1 tablespoon rice wine and ½ teaspoon sugar in medium bowl; stir in liver. Sprinkle with 1 tablespoon cornstarch; stir to mix well. Stir in 1 teaspoon sesame oil. Marinate at room temperature 30 minutes.

3. Pour boiling water over chili peppers in small bowl; let stand 5 minutes. Drain and pat dry. Break cloud ears into 1½-inch pieces.

4. Cut onions into 1¼-inch lengths. Cut celery diagonally into ¼-inch thick slices. Mix 1 teaspoon cornstarch and the cold water in small bowl until smooth; stir in rice vinegar, 1 tablespoon each soy sauce and rice wine and ½ teaspoon sugar.

5. Heat wok over high heat 15 seconds; add 3 tablespoons peanut oil and heat until hot, about 30 seconds. Scatter in liver, ¼ at a time; stir-fry just until liver changes color, about 1 minute after all liver has been added. Transfer liver to plate.

6. Wipe wok clean; add 2 tablespoons peanut oil and heat until hot. Reduce heat to medium; stir-fry ginger and chili peppers 10 seconds. Increase heat to high and scatter in celery; stir-fry 1½ minutes. Add onions; stir-fry 30 seconds. Stir in liver and cloud ears. Stir cornstarch mixture

and add to wok; cook and stir until sauce thickens, about 30 seconds. Drizzle with 1 teaspoon sesame oil; stir 3 or 4 times. Serve immediately.

Makes 3 or 4 servings

Pork with Bean Sauce

1 pound boneless pork loin
1 small egg
2½ tablespoons rice wine
2½ tablespoons soy sauce
Pinch pepper
1½ tablespoons plus 2
  teaspoons cornstarch
3 tablespoons plus 2
  teaspoons peanut oil
3 green onions, white part
  only
¼ cup ground brown bean
  sauce
1 tablespoon sugar
2 tablespoons cold water
1½ cups vegetable oil
1½ teaspoons minced pared
  fresh ginger root
⅔ cup chicken stock or broth
1 package (10 ounces) frozen
  peas, thawed and drained

1. Cut pork lengthwise, with the grain, into ½-inch thick slices. Score one side of each slice with cleaver or chef's knife, making narrowly spaced cuts diagonal to the grain and cutting ⅔ of the

way through meat. Make second set of diagonal cuts in opposite direction of first set, to form criss-cross pattern. Turn slices over and cut with the grain into ¾-inch wide strips; cut strips crosswise into ¾-inch squares.

2. Beat egg, 1 tablespoon each rice wine and soy sauce and the pepper in medium bowl; stir in pork. Sprinkle with 1½ tablespoons cornstarch; stir to mix well. Stir in 1 tablespoon peanut oil. Marinate at room temperature 30 minutes.

3. Cut onions into ½-inch pieces. Mix bean sauce, sugar and 1½ tablespoons each rice wine and soy sauce in small bowl. Mix 2 teaspoons cornstarch in the water in a cup until smooth.

4. Heat wok over high heat 20 seconds; add vegetable oil and heat to 375°F. Reduce heat to medium low. Using ¼ of the pork at a time, add to wok and immediately stir with quick but gentle circular motion to separate pieces. Cook and stir until coating is firm and golden, 30 to 45 seconds. Remove pork with strainer; drain on paper toweling. Reheat oil to 375°F and repeat with remaining pork. Remove oil from wok; wipe clean.

5. Heat wok over high heat 15 seconds; add 2 tablespoons peanut oil and heat until hot, about 30 seconds. Reduce heat to medium. Add bean sauce

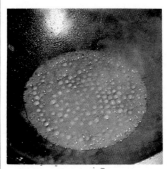

mixture; cook and stir until sauce is smooth and shiny, about 1 minute.

6. Add onions, ginger and stock to wok; heat over high heat to boiling. Stir in peas; heat to boiling. Reduce heat to medium-high. Stir in pork; cook and stir 1 minute. Stir cornstarch mixture and add to wok; cook and stir until sauce thickens, about 10 seconds. Drizzle with 2 teaspoons peanut oil; stir 3 or 4 times. Serve immediately.

Makes 4 servings

Twice-Cooked Pork with Cabbage

1 pound boneless pork loin
  blade (rib end)*
½ pound green cabbage
2 medium green bell peppers
4 green onions, white part
  only
3 tablespoons brown bean
  sauce
2 tablespoons soy sauce
1 tablespoon rice wine
2 teaspoons sugar
1 to 3 teaspoons chili paste
  with garlic
6 tablespoons peanut oil
1 teaspoon minced pared
  fresh ginger root
1 clove garlic, minced

Leave fat untrimmed for flavor and juiciness; trim after cooking and chilling, if desired.

1. Cook and chill pork following directions in Steps 1, 2 and 3 of "White-Cut Pork" (see Index for page number), except do not reserve cooking liquid. Cut pork across the grain into ⅛-inch thick slices.

2. Core and separate cabbage leaves; cut leaves into 2-inch triangles. Cut peppers lengthwise into 1-inch wide strips; cut strips diagonally in half lengthwise to form triangles. Slant-cut onions into ½-inch lengths.

3. Mix bean sauce, soy sauce, rice wine, sugar and chili paste in small bowl.

4. Heat wok over high heat 15 seconds; add 3 tablespoons oil and heat until hot, about 30 seconds. Scatter in cabbage, peppers and onions, about ⅓ at a time; stir-fry just until vegetables begin to wilt, 1½ to 2 minutes after all are added. Transfer mixture to plate.

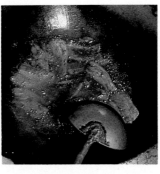

5. Add 3 tablespoons oil to wok; heat over high heat until hot. Scatter in pork; stir-fry until light brown, 2 to 3 minutes. Add ginger and garlic; stir-fry 10 seconds. Add bean sauce mixture; cook and stir 30 seconds. Return vegetables to wok; cook and stir until vegetables are tender and coated with slightly thickened sauce, about 1 minute. Serve immediately.

Makes 4 servings

Beef with Fried Noodles

¾ pound boneless top sirloin
½ pound dried Chinese egg
    noodles
3 quarts boiling water
½ teaspoon salt
8 to 9 tablespoons plus 2
    teaspoons peanut oil
3 tablespoons soy sauce
1½ tablespoons rice wine
1½ teaspoons sugar
½ teaspoon minced garlic
2 tablespoons plus 2
    teaspoons cornstarch
3 tablespoons cold water
2 cups chicken stock or broth
3 ounces frozen snow peas,
    thawed and drained
1 cup canned straw
    mushrooms, rinsed and
    drained
⅔ cup canned baby corn,
    rinsed and drained
2 tablespoons minced green
    onion, white part only
2 teaspoons minced pared
    fresh ginger root

1. To facilitate slicing, freeze beef until firm, not frozen, 30 to 40 minutes. Cook noodles in boiling water in kettle until firm-tender, 3 to 6 minutes after water returns to boiling. Drain noodles; rinse under cold running water. Drain well. Sprinkle with salt; drizzle with 1 tablespoon oil. Mix with hands to coat noodles; reserve, uncovered, at room temperature.

2. Cut beef across the grain into ⅛-inch thick slices. Stack slices; cut into 1½×1-inch pieces. Combine beef, 1 tablespoon soy sauce, ½ tablespoon rice wine, 1 teaspoon sugar and the garlic; stir to mix well. Stir in 2 teaspoons cornstarch; mix well. Stir in 2 teaspoons oil. Marinate at room temperature 30 minutes.

3. Mix 2 tablespoons cornstarch and the cold water until smooth. Stir in stock, 2 tablespoons soy sauce, 1 tablespoon rice wine and ½ teaspoon sugar.

4. Heat wok over high heat 15 seconds; add 3 tablespoons oil and heat until hot, about 30 seconds. Add ¼ of noodles at

a time to wok, shaping into flat nests. Press noodles with spatula to flatten. Fry 10 seconds; reduce heat to medium-low and fry without stir-

ring until brown and crisp, about 4 minutes per side. (Add 1 tablespoon oil around edge of noodles if needed.) Transfer to serving platter; keep warm in 200°F oven.

5. Add 1 tablespoon oil to wok; heat over high heat until hot. Add snow peas; stir-fry 15 seconds. Remove to plate. Add 2 tablespoons oil to wok and heat until hot. Scatter in beef, ⅓ at a time; stir-fry 1 minute after all beef is added. Remove to plate.

6. Add 1 tablespoon oil to wok; heat until hot. Add mushrooms and corn; stir-fry 45 seconds. Add onion and ginger; stir-fry 10 seconds. Stir cornstarch mixture and add to wok; heat to boiling. Return

beef and snow peas to wok. Cook and stir until sauce is thickened, 1 minute. Pour beef mixture over noodles.
Makes 4 to 6 servings

Stuffed Black Mushrooms

4 extra-large (4-inch) dried
   black Chinese
   mushrooms*
¾ pound ground pork
1 large egg, lightly beaten
2½ tablespoons rice wine
2 tablespoons soy sauce
¼ teaspoon salt
Pinch pepper
5 tablespoons cornstarch
1 pound fresh spinach
2 green onions
1⅓ cups chicken stock or
   broth
1¼ teaspoons sugar
Boiling water
¾ cup vegetable oil
2 teaspoons minced pared
   fresh ginger root
2 tablespoons cold water
2 tablespoons oyster sauce
3 tablespoons peanut oil

*Recipe will fill about 8 large
(3-inch) or 12 medium (2-inch)
mushrooms.*

1. Soften and clean mushrooms. Strain and reserve ⅔ cup soaking liquid.

2. Mix thoroughly pork, egg, 1 tablespoon each rice wine and soy sauce, the salt and pepper in medium bowl. Add 2 tablespoons cornstarch; mix well. Refrigerate 15 minutes.

3. Clean and trim spinach, leaving 1½ inches stems attached. Cut onions into 2-inch lengths. Mix stock, soaking liquid, 1½ tablespoons rice wine, 1 tablespoon soy sauce and the sugar in small bowl.

4. Add mushrooms to boiling water in small saucepan; boil 2 minutes. Drain; rinse with cold water. Squeeze gently; press between several layers paper toweling to remove moisture. Place 1 tablespoon cornstarch on saucer. Press underside of mushrooms into cornstarch to coat; shake off excess.

5. Divide meat mixture evenly among mushrooms; place meat on underside of each mushroom. Dip fingers into 1

tablespoon cornstarch; pat meat to extend slightly beyond mushroom edges. Dust meat with the cornstarch.

6. Heat wok over high heat 20 seconds; add vegetable oil and heat to 350°F. Fry 4 mushrooms at a time, meat-side-down, until light brown, 2 to 3 minutes. Turn mushrooms over; fry 2 minutes. Remove with slotted spoon; drain on paper toweling. Remove oil from wok; wipe clean.

7. Arrange mushrooms in single layer in wok, meat-

side-down. Add stock mixture, onions and ginger; heat to boiling. Adjust heat for low simmer; simmer, covered, 30 minutes. Remove mushrooms with slotted spoon to serving bowl; keep warm. Cook stock mixture, uncovered, over medium-high heat until reduced to 1 cup, 3 to 4 minutes. Remove and discard onions. Mix 1 tablespoon cornstarch and the cold water in cup until smooth; stir into stock mixture. Cook and stir until sauce thickens, about 30 seconds. Stir in oyster sauce. Pour sauce over mushrooms. Clean wok.

8. Heat wok over high heat 15 seconds; add peanut oil and heat until hot, about 30 seconds. Add spinach. (Stand back from wok when adding spinach; oil may spatter.) Stir-fry just until spinach is bright green and wilted, about 1 minute. Arrange around mushrooms.

Makes 3 to 4 servings

Shredded Pork and Napa

¾ pound boneless pork loin
3 tablespoons soy sauce
1 large egg white, lightly
   beaten
1 tablespoon cornstarch
5 tablespoons peanut oil
22 ounces napa (preferably
   near root end)
2 tablespoons salt
¼ cup water
2 green onions, white part
   only
1 to 3 dried red chili peppers,
   seeded
1 tablespoon rice wine
2 teaspoons Chinese black
   vinegar
2 teaspoons sugar
3 cups vegetable oil
2 teaspoons minced pared
   fresh ginger root

1. Freeze pork until firm but not frozen, 30 to 40 minutes. Cut pork across the grain into ⅛-inch thick slices. Arrange slices slightly overlapping; roll up jelly-roll style. Cut crosswise into ⅛-inch wide shreds.

2. Combine pork with 1 tablespoon soy sauce in medium bowl; stir in egg white. Sprinkle with cornstarch; stir to mix well. Stir in 1 tablespoon peanut oil; refrigerate, covered, 30 minutes to 1 hour.

3. Meanwhile, separate napa leaves; cut crosswise into 4-

inch lengths. Stack leaves; cut lengthwise into ⅛-inch wide shreds. Place in large bowl; sprinkle with salt and toss. Drizzle with the water. Top napa with a plate and 3-pound weight. Let stand 30 minutes.

4. Cut onions and chili peppers separately into ½-inch pieces. Mix 2 tablespoons soy sauce, the rice wine, vinegar and sugar in small bowl. Rinse napa thoroughly to remove salt; drain well. Spread on paper toweling; pat dry.

5. Heat wok over high heat 20 seconds; add vegetable oil and heat to 350°F. Reduce heat to medium; stir pork to loosen. Add ½ of pork to wok; stir gently. Fry just until pork changes color, 30 to 45 seconds. Remove with strainer; drain on paper toweling. Reheat oil to 350°F and repeat with remaining pork. Remove oil from wok; wipe clean.

6. Heat wok over high heat 15 seconds; add 4 tablespoons peanut oil and heat until hot, about 30 seconds. Reduce heat to low. Add chili peppers; stir-fry until dark red, about 10 seconds. Add onions and ginger; stir-fry 10 seconds.

7. Increase heat to high. Scatter napa into wok; stir-fry 1½ minutes. Add pork; stir-fry 30 seconds. Add soy sauce mixture; cook and stir until ingredients are coated, about 30 seconds. Serve immediately.

Makes 3 servings

Stir-Fried Garlic Pork

¾ **pound boneless pork shoulder**
⅛ **ounce dried cloud ears, softened and cleaned**
½ **pound pickled mustard green, drained***
4 **ounces canned bamboo shoots, rinsed and drained**
8 **green onions, white part only**
5 **tablespoons peanut oil**
2 **teaspoons minced pared fresh ginger root**
1 **large clove garlic, minced**
2 **tablespoons soy sauce**
2 **tablespoons rice wine**
1 **teaspoon sugar**
½ **to 1 teaspoon sesame chili oil, if desired**

Any pickled Chinese vegetable can be used.

1. Freeze pork until firm, not frozen, 30 to 40 minutes. Break cloud ears into 1-inch pieces. Separate pieces of mustard green and stack 2 or 3 at a time. Cut lengthwise into

1-inch wide strips; slant-cut strips into 1-inch squares. Soak in bowl of cold water 5 minutes. Drain well; pat dry.

2. Cut pork across the grain into ⅛-inch thick slices; stack slices and cut into 1¼-inch squares. Cut bamboo shoots into ¼-inch thick slices; cut slices into 1-inch pieces. Cut onions into 1-inch lengths.

3. Heat wok over high heat 15 seconds; add 3 tablespoons peanut oil and heat until hot, about 30 seconds. Reduce heat to medium; stir-fry ginger and garlic 10 seconds. Increase heat to high. Add bamboo shoots; stir-fry 15 seconds. Add green onions; stir-fry 10 seconds. Add mustard green; stir-fry 30 seconds. Stir in 1 tablespoon each soy sauce and rice wine; stir-fry 15 seconds. Transfer vegetable mixture to plate.

4. Add 2 tablespoons peanut oil to wok; heat over high heat until hot. Scatter in pork, ⅓ at a time; stir fry 1½ minutes

after all pork is added. Add 1 tablespoon each soy sauce and rice wine and the sugar; cook and stir 10 seconds. Add stir-fried vegetables and cloud ears; cook and stir 1 minute. Cover wok and steam-cook 30 seconds. Stir in sesame chili oil. Serve immediately.
Makes 3 servings

Chili Pork with Bean Threads

4 **ounces bean threads**
3 **tablespoons ground brown bean sauce**
3 **tablespoons rice wine**
3 **tablespoons soy sauce**
4 **tablespoons peanut oil**
1 **tablespoon minced pared fresh ginger root**
½ **teaspoon minced garlic**
¾ **pound ground pork or beef, march-chopped**
1 **to 2 teaspoons chili paste with garlic, if desired**
2 **to 3 cups chicken stock or broth**
⅓ **cup chopped green onion, white part only**
⅛ **teaspoon pepper**

1. Soak bean threads in large bowl of hot tap water 10 minutes. Cut into 4-inch lengths

with scissors; drain. Soak cut bean threads in cold water 20 minutes; drain well.

2. Mix bean sauce, rice wine and 2 tablespoons soy sauce in small bowl until smooth.

3. Heat wok over high heat 15 seconds; add 3 tablespoons oil and heat until hot, about 30 seconds. Reduce heat to medium; stir-fry ginger and garlic 10 seconds. Increase heat to high. Scatter in pork, about ⅓ at a time; stir-fry, breaking up meat into fine pieces with spatula, until pork changes color, about 1 minute after all pork has been added.

Add bean sauce mixture; stir-fry 30 seconds. Stir in chili paste. Add bean thread; stir-fry 1 minute.

4. Add 2 cups stock to wok; heat to boiling. Add onions and 1 tablespoon soy sauce. Reduce heat to medium; simmer, stirring frequently, 4 minutes. (Bean threads absorb liquid during cooking.) As mixture begins to dry out, add ¼ cup stock as needed. Mixture should be moist with some visible liquid remaining when cooking is finished.

5. Drizzle with 1 tablespoon oil; stir 3 to 4 times. Sprinkle with pepper. Serve immediately.

Makes 4 to 6 servings

Pork and Potato Patties

1 pound Idaho potatoes or
  sweet potatoes, pared
2 ounces Canadian bacon or
  ham
3 medium dried black
  Chinese mushrooms,
  softened and cleaned
½ pound ground pork,
  march-chopped
2 tablespoons minced green
  onion, white part only
2 teaspoons minced pared
  fresh ginger root
1 large egg
2½ tablespoons rice wine
Pinch pepper
3 tablespoons plus 2
  teaspoons cornstarch
¼ cup plus 1 teaspoon peanut
  oil
3 green onions, white part
  only
2 cups chicken stock or broth
1 tablespoon soy sauce
1 tablespoon cold water

1. Dice potatoes into ¼-inch
cubes; rinse in cold water and
drain well. Mince bacon and
mushrooms.

2. Combine pork, potatoes,
bacon, mushrooms, minced
onion and ginger in large
bowl. Add egg, 1½ table-
spoons rice wine and the pepper; mix well. Sprinkle with 3
tablespoons cornstarch; mix

well. Shape mixture, packing
tightly, into 2 × ½-inch patties.

3. Heat wok over high heat 15
seconds; add ¼ cup oil and
heat until hot, about 30 seconds. Reduce heat to medium-low. Place patties in single
layer in wok; cook, turning
once, until light brown, 2½ to
3 minutes per side. (Patties in
center will cook faster than
those around edges; rearrange
as needed for even cooking.)
Remove patties to plate. Discard oil; wipe wok clean.

4. Cut 3 onions into ½-inch
pieces. Combine onions,
stock, soy sauce and 1 tablespoon rice wine in wok. Heat

over high heat to boiling; add
patties in single layer. Reduce
heat to maintain low boil; cook
until patties are cooked
through and liquid is reduced
by half, 15 to 20 minutes.
Transfer patties with slotted
spoon to serving dish.

5. Mix 2 teaspoons cornstarch
with cold water until smooth;
stir into wok. Cook and stir
over high heat until sauce
thickens and bubbles for 1
minute. Remove onions with
slotted spoon; discard. Stir 1
teaspoon oil into sauce; pour
over patties. Serve immediately.

Makes 4 servings

Beef Tenderloin with Onions

1 pound beef tenderloin
1 small egg
4 tablespoons rice wine
2 teaspoons sugar
2½ tablespoons cornstarch
6 tablespoons peanut oil
4 medium yellow onions
1 large clove garlic
¼ cup cold water
3 tablespoons soy sauce
⅛ teaspoon pepper
2 teaspoons sesame oil

1. To facilitate slicing, freeze beef until firm but not frozen, 30 to 45 minutes. Cut beef across the grain into ⅛-inch thick slices. Stack slices; cut into ⅛-inch wide strips. Wet knife in cold water as needed to prevent sticking.

2. Beat egg, 1 tablespoon rice wine and ½ teaspoon sugar in medium bowl; stir in beef. Sprinkle with 1½ tablespoons cornstarch; stir to mix well. Stir in 1 tablespoon peanut oil. Marinate at room temperature 30 minutes.

3. Cut onions lengthwise in half; cut halves crosswise into ⅛-inch thick slices. Lightly pound garlic with flat side of cleaver.

4. Mix 1 tablespoon cornstarch with the water in small bowl until smooth; stir in 3 tablespoons rice wine, 1½ teaspoons sugar, the soy sauce and pepper.

5. Heat wok over high heat 15 seconds; add 2 tablespoons peanut oil and heat until hot, about 30 seconds. Scatter in

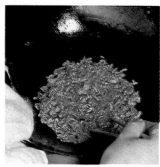

Scatter in beef, ¼ at a time, and stir-fry just until beef is no longer red, 1½ to 2 minutes after all beef has been added. Discard garlic. Return onions to wok; stir-fry 15 seconds.

onions; stir-fry until onions begin to turn translucent but not limp, 1 to 1½ minutes. Transfer onions to plate.

6. Add 3 tablespoons peanut oil to wok; heat until hot. Add garlic; stir and press against bottom of wok 10 seconds.

7. Stir soy-sauce mixture and add to wok. Cook and stir until sauce thickens, 20 to 30 seconds. Drizzle with sesame oil; stir 3 or 4 times. Serve immediately.

Makes 4 servings

White-Cut Pork

1 pound boneless pork loin blade (rib end)*
4 to 5 cups boiling water
Ice cubes
1 teaspoon Szechuan peppercorns, if desired
½ cup soy sauce
5 tablespoons rice wine
1 tablespoon sugar
1 tablespoon Chinese black vinegar
1 to 2 teaspoons sesame oil, if desired
1 teaspoon minced garlic
½ to 1 teaspoon chili oil, if desired
12 ounces "seedless" thin cucumbers
3 thin slices fresh ginger root
2 green onions

Leave fat untrimmed for flavor and juiciness; trim after cooking and chilling, if desired.

1. Rinse pork; place in wok. Add boiling water to cover. Heat over high heat to boiling; boil 2 minutes. Adjust heat to maintain strong simmer, medium-low. Skim foam;

cover wok. Cook until juices run clear when pork is pierced to center with knife, about 1 hour. Check occasionally; add boiling water if needed to cover pork. Turn pork after 30 minutes.

2. Fill large bowl halfway with cold water. Place cooked pork in water; add ice cubes to cover. Let stand 20 minutes. Reserve cooking liquid in wok.

3. Remove pork from cold water; pat dry. Wrap in plastic wrap; refrigerate at least 1 hour.

4. Dry-roast peppercorns in small skillet over low heat, shaking occasionally, until fragrant, 5 minutes. Cool; crush in mortar with pestle or in bowl with end of cleaver handle.

5. Mix soy sauce, 3 tablespoons rice wine and the sugar in saucepan. Heat over

medium heat to simmering. Transfer to bowl; cool. Stir in vinegar, sesame oil, garlic and chili oil.

6. About 20 minutes before serving, cut cucumbers lengthwise into paper-thin slices. Soak in bowl of cold water 5 minutes. Cut pork across the grain into 1/16-inch thick slices.

7. Pare ginger root. Pound onions and ginger with flat side of cleaver; add to cooking liquid reserved in wok. Add 2 tablespoons rice wine; heat to boiling.

8. Drain cucumbers; arrange evenly on serving platter.

9. Turn off heat under boiling cooking liquid. Immediately add pork slices and stir; let stand just to warm, 15 sec-

onds. Remove pork with strainer, draining well; place on top of cucumbers. Add peppercorns to soy sauce mixture and serve as dipping sauce or dressing to spoon over pork and cucumbers.

Makes 3 to 4 servings

Chicken

Sweet and Sour Chicken

1¼ pounds chicken thighs (about 5)
1 large egg, separated
2 tablespoons soy sauce
¼ cup plus ½ teaspoon sugar
¾ teaspoon salt
Pinch black pepper
½ cup plus 2 tablespoons cornstarch
2 large green bell peppers
1 small clove garlic
½ cup chicken stock or broth
3 tablespoons distilled white vinegar
2 tablespoons rice wine
½ cup water
½ cup all-purpose flour
4 cups vegetable oil
3 tablespoons peanut oil
1½ cups fresh or canned drained pineapple chunks (about ⅜×1 inch)
1 tablespoon sesame oil

1. Bone chicken thighs following directions in Steps 2 and 3 of "Chicken Stir-Fry with Radish" (see Index for page number); remove and discard skin if desired. Cut chicken into ¾-inch pieces. Mix egg yolk, 1 tablespoon soy sauce, ½ teaspoon each sugar and salt and the black pepper in medium bowl; stir in chicken. Sprinkle with 1 tablespoon cornstarch; stir to mix well. Marinate at room temperature 30 minutes.

2. Cut green peppers into 1¼-inch pieces. Lightly pound garlic with flat side of cleaver.

3. Mix 1 tablespoon cornstarch with ¼ cup sugar and ¼ teaspoon salt in small bowl. Stir in stock, vinegar, rice wine and 1 tablespoon soy sauce.

4. Whisk egg white in medium bowl until foamy and double in volume; whisk in water. Whisk in ½ cup cornstarch until smooth; whisk in flour until smooth. Reserve batter.

5. Heat wok over high heat 20 seconds; add vegetable oil and heat to 350°F. Using ⅓ of chicken pieces at a time, dip each piece in batter and add to wok. Stir gently. Fry until

crisp, golden and cooked through, 4 to 5 minutes. Remove chicken with strainer; drain on paper toweling. Reheat oil to 350°F and repeat with remaining chicken. Remove oil from wok; wipe clean.

6. Heat wok over high heat 15 seconds; add 2 tablespoons peanut oil and heat until hot, about 30 seconds. Scatter in green peppers and garlic and stir-fry 2 minutes; remove with slotted spoon to plate. Discard garlic.

7. Add 1 tablespoon peanut oil to wok; heat until hot. Reduce heat to medium. Add pineapple; stir-fry 30 seconds. Stir stock mixture; add to wok. Increase heat to high; cook and stir until sauce thickens and bubbles for 1 minute. Drizzle with sesame oil; stir 2 or 3 times. Return green peppers and chicken to wok and stir just until coated with sauce. Serve immediately.

Makes 4 servings

Red-Cooked Chicken

2 pounds chicken thighs
5 tablespoons soy sauce
1 can (19 ounces) young or "green" bamboo shoots, rinsed and drained
1 green onion
2 thin slices fresh ginger root
4 cups vegetable oil
3 tablespoons sugar
1 cup plus 1½ tablespoons cold water
1 tablespoon peanut oil
¾ cup chicken stock or broth
¼ cup rice wine
1 star anise
1-inch piece cinnamon stick
⅛ teaspoon pepper
2½ teaspoons cornstarch

1. Cut chicken thighs crosswise in half with cleaver. Place chicken in medium bowl; rub with 2 tablespoons soy sauce to coat. Marinate at room temperature 15 minutes.

2. Roll-cut bamboo shoots into 1½-inch pieces. Drain well on paper toweling. Pat chicken dry with paper toweling. Cut onion crosswise in half. Pare ginger root. Pound onion and ginger lightly with flat side of cleaver.

3. Heat wok over high heat 20 seconds; add vegetable oil and heat to 375°F. Fry chicken, ½ at a time, over high heat 2½ minutes; remove with strainer to plate. Fry bamboo shoots 45 seconds; remove with strainer to plate. Remove oil from wok; wipe clean.

4. Have sugar and 1 cup cold water next to wok. Heat wok over high heat 15 seconds; add peanut oil and heat 30 seconds. Reduce heat to medium. Add sugar; cook and stir until sugar melts and turns dark brown, about 1 minute. Watch closely and do not allow sugar to burn. Stand as far from wok as possible; immediately add the cold water; stir. (Sugar will spatter when water is added.)

5. Add chicken and bamboo shoots to wok; spread in even layer. Add chicken stock, rice wine, 3 tablespoons soy sauce, the onion, ginger, star anise, cinnamon stick and pepper. Heat over high heat to boiling; reduce heat to maintain strong simmer, about medium-low. Cook, covered, until chicken is very tender, about 30 minutes.

6. Remove chicken and bamboo shoots from wok to serving bowl with slotted spoon. Remove and discard onion, ginger, star anise and cinnamon stick. Mix cornstarch and 1½ tablespoons cold water in a cup until smooth; stir into cooking liquid in wok. Cook and stir over high heat until sauce thickens, about 1 minute. Pour over chicken and bamboo shoots. Serve immediately.

Makes 4 to 6 servings

Fried Chicken with Ginger Dressing

4 chicken legs with thighs attached (about 2½ pounds)
1 teaspoon salt
⅛ teaspoon white pepper
2 green onions
3 thin slices fresh ginger root
2 tablespoons rice wine
3 cups shredded iceberg lettuce
¼ cup sugar
¼ cup rice vinegar
3 tablespoons chicken stock or broth
2 tablespoons soy sauce
1 tablespoon sesame oil
⅓ cup minced green onion, white part only
2 tablespoons minced pared fresh ginger root
2 tablespoons minced fresh parsley
1 small egg white
4 tablespoons cornstarch
4 cups vegetable oil

1. Sprinkle chicken with salt and pepper; rub to coat evenly. Place chicken in nonaluminum baking pan. Pound 2 onions and the sliced ginger root lightly with flat side of cleaver; chop coarsely and scatter over chicken. Sprinkle chicken with rice wine. Marinate at room temperature, turning chicken once, 30 minutes.

2. Arrange lettuce on large serving platter. Refrigerate covered.

3. Mix sugar, vinegar, stock, soy sauce and sesame oil in small saucepan. Stir in minced onion, ginger and parsley.

4. Whisk egg white in small bowl until foamy and double in volume. Whisk in 2 tablespoons cornstarch. Reserve batter.

5. Heat wok over high heat 20 seconds; add vegetable oil and heat to 350°F.

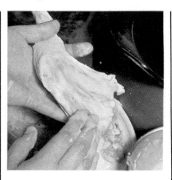

6. Meanwhile, drain chicken; discard marinade. Pat chicken dry with paper toweling; dust with 2 tablespoons cornstarch. Spread batter on areas of chicken *not* covered with skin, coating evenly.

7. Fry 2 chicken pieces at a time, turning once, until crispy and cooked through, 7 to 9 minutes. (To test for doneness, pierce thickest part of drumstick to the bone with tip of knife; juices should run clear.) Drain chicken on paper toweling; keep warm in 200°F oven. Repeat, frying remaining 2 chicken pieces.

8. Heat stock mixture over medium heat to simmering. Reduce heat to low; simmer 1 minute. Keep dressing hot.

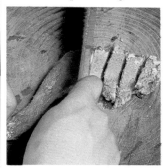

9. Cut warm chicken into ½-inch wide slices; use a meat mallet or hammer to pound cleaver or sturdy chef's knife through bones. Reassemble chicken slices and place on bed of lettuce. Pour hot dressing over chicken. Serve immediately.

Makes 4 servings

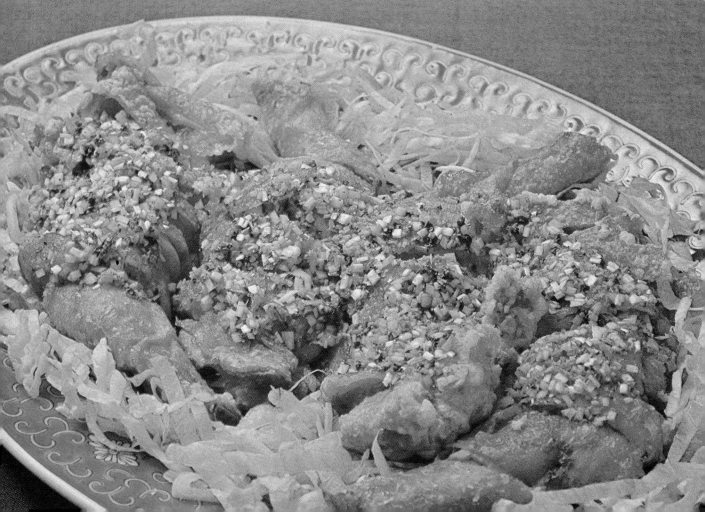

Kung Pao Chicken

1¼ pounds chicken thighs
(about 5)
1 small egg
1½ tablespoons plus 2
teaspoons cornstarch
4 tablespoons soy sauce
4 tablespoons peanut oil
1 can (19 ounces) bamboo
shoots, rinsed and drained
8 green onions, white part
only
3 to 5 dried red chili peppers,
seeded
1½ tablespoons cold water
2 tablespoons rice wine
1½ tablespoons Chinese
black vinegar
1 tablespoon plus 1 teaspoon
sugar
2 teaspoons sesame oil
1 teaspoon minced pared
fresh ginger root
1 small clove garlic, minced
1 cup unsalted roasted
peanuts

1. Bone chicken thighs following directions in Steps 2 and 3 of "Chicken Stir-Fry with Radish" (see Index for page number); remove and discard skin if desired. Cut chicken into ¾-inch pieces. Beat egg in medium bowl; add

chicken. Sprinkle with 1½ tablespoons cornstarch; mix well. Stir in 1 tablespoon each soy sauce and peanut oil. Marinate at room temperature 30 minutes.

2. Cut bamboo shoots into ¾-inch cubes. Cut onions into ¾-inch pieces. Cut peppers into ½-inch pieces.

3. Mix 2 teaspoons cornstarch and the water in small bowl until smooth. Stir in 3 tablespoons soy sauce, the rice wine, vinegar, sugar and sesame oil.

4. Heat wok over high heat 15 seconds; add 3 tablespoons peanut oil and heat until hot, about 30 seconds. Reduce heat to low. Add peppers; cook, stirring and pressing peppers against wok, until dark red, about 10 seconds. Add ginger and garlic; stir-fry 10 seconds. Increase heat to high. Scatter in chicken, about ¼ at a time; stir-fry 1 minute after all

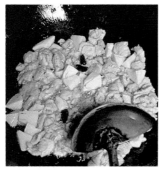

chicken has been added. Add bamboo shoots; stir-fry 1 minute. Add onions; stir-fry 30 seconds.

5. Stir cornstarch mixture; add to wok. Cook and stir until sauce thickens and coats chicken evenly, about 30 sec-

onds. Add peanuts and turn off heat; stir mixture 2 or 3 times. Serve immediately.
Makes 4 servings

Chicken and Asparagus in Oyster Sauce

1 pound skinned and boned
  chicken breasts
2 tablespoons rice wine
¼ teaspoon salt
1 large egg white
1 tablespoon plus 2 teaspoons
  cornstarch
4 tablespoons peanut oil
1 pound fresh asparagus
¼ cup cold chicken stock or
  broth
3 tablespoons oyster sauce
1 tablespoon soy sauce
2 teaspoons rice vinegar
1 teaspoon sugar
2 cups vegetable oil
¼ cup coarsely chopped
  green onion
2 teaspoons minced pared
  fresh ginger root

1. Pound each chicken piece lightly with flat side of cleaver to flatten slightly. Cut chicken lengthwise into ¼-inch wide strips. Cut strips crosswise into 2- to 2½-inch lengths.

2. Combine chicken, 1 tablespoon rice wine and the salt in medium bowl. Beat egg white

very lightly in small bowl. Stir into chicken mixture. Sprinkle with 1 tablespoon cornstarch; stir until smooth. Stir in 1 tablespoon peanut oil; refrigerate, covered, 30 minutes to 1 hour.

3. Cut off asparagus tips. If stalks are thicker than ½ inch in diameter, cut lengthwise in half. Cut stalks crosswise into 2½-inch lengths.

4. Mix 2 teaspoons cornstarch and the chicken stock in small bowl until smooth. Stir in oys-

ter sauce, soy sauce, vinegar, sugar and 1 tablespoon rice wine.

5. Heat wok over high heat 20 seconds; add vegetable oil and heat over medium heat to 275°F. Velvet ⅓ of chicken at a time: Stir chicken; add to wok. Stir gently. Cook just until chicken turns white on the outside but is still raw in center, 30 to 45 seconds. Remove

chicken with strainer; drain on paper toweling. Reheat oil to 275°F and repeat with remaining chicken. Remove oil from wok; wipe clean.

6. Heat wok over high heat 15 seconds; add 3 tablespoons peanut oil and heat until hot, about 30 seconds. Reduce heat to medium; stir-fry onion and ginger 10 seconds. Increase heat to high and scatter in asparagus tips and stalks, ¼ at a time; stir-fry just until asparagus begins to soften, 2 to

3 minutes. Scatter in chicken; stir-fry 1 minute. Stir stock mixture and add to wok; cook and stir until sauce is thickened, about 30 seconds. Serve immediately.

Makes 4 servings

Chicken Stir-Fry with Radish

2 medium dried black
  Chinese mushrooms
1¼ pounds chicken thighs
  (about 5)
2 tablespoons plus 2
  teaspoons rice wine
¾ teaspoon sugar
1 tablespoon cornstarch
6 ounces pickled radish,
  drained
6 ounces fresh white button
  mushrooms
1 tablespoon ground brown
  bean sauce
2 teaspoons soy sauce
¼ cup peanut oil
⅓ cup chopped green onion,
  white part only

1. Soften and clean black mushrooms. Strain and reserve 3 tablespoons of the soaking liquid.

2. To bone chicken thighs: Place thigh skin-side-down; probe with fingers to locate bone. Make 1 cut through the meat to the bone. Scrape meat

away from bone with tip of knife, working from center out to ends of bone.

3. At ends of bone, scrape and pull meat away from bone,

cartilage and tendons; detach meat with knife or scissors. Pull off and discard skin.

4. Dice chicken into ⅜-inch cubes. Mix chicken with 2 tablespoons rice wine and the sugar in medium bowl. Sprinkle with cornstarch; stir to mix well. Marinate at room temperature 30 minutes.

5. Dice pickled radish into ¼-inch cubes; soak in large bowl of cold water to remove excess salt, 20 minutes. Drain well. Clean and trim white mushrooms. Dice white and black mushrooms into ¼-inch

cubes. Mix bean sauce, soy sauce, 2 teaspoons rice wine and the reserved mushroom soaking liquid in small bowl.

6. Heat wok over high heat 15 seconds; add peanut oil and heat until hot, about 30 sec-

onds. Scatter in chicken ¼ at a time; stir-fry 30 seconds after all chicken is added. Scatter in white and black mushrooms; stir-fry 30 seconds. Add pickled radish; stir-fry 1 minute. Stir in bean sauce mixture and onions; cook and stir 15 seconds. Serve immediately.

Makes 3 to 4 servings

48

Pang Pang Chicken

2 whole chicken breasts (about 14 ounces each)
1½ to 2 quarts boiling water
Ice cubes
3 medium cucumbers, preferably unwaxed
¼ cup sesame paste
1 to 3 teaspoons sesame oil
3 tablespoons minced green onion, white part only
1 tablespoon sugar
2 teaspoons minced pared fresh ginger root
2 teaspoons Chinese black vinegar
¼ teaspoon minced garlic, if desired
2 tablespoons soy sauce
¼ to ½ teaspoon hot pepper oil, if desired

1. Rinse chicken; place in wok. Add boiling water to cover. Heat over high heat to boiling. Adjust heat to maintain strong simmer or low boil, about medium-low. Skim foam; cover wok. Cook until juices run clear when chicken is pierced in thickest part with a knife, 20 to 25 minutes. Turn chicken over after first 10 minutes.

2. Fill large bowl halfway with cold water. Add chicken. Quickly add ice cubes to cover; let stand 20 minutes. Remove chicken from water; pat dry. Wrap in plastic wrap; refrigerate at least 2 hours or overnight.

3. About 30 minutes before serving, cut cucumbers crosswise into 2½-inch lengths. Pound each piece fairly hard with flat side of cleaver; cucumber will split lengthwise into 3 or 4 pieces. Break pieces apart completely, and remove seeds. Cut pieces lengthwise into ¼-inch wide sticks. Arrange on dish.

4. Pull chicken meat away from bones in 1 piece, leaving skin intact. Cut chicken lengthwise into ¼-inch thick slices; arrange overlapping on top of cucumbers.

5. Mix sesame paste and sesame oil in small bowl until smooth; amount of oil needed depends on thickness of sesame paste. Add onion, sugar, ginger, vinegar and garlic; drizzle with soy sauce and stir to mix well. Stir in hot pepper oil. Spoon sesame sauce over chicken. Serve immediately.

Makes 4 to 6 servings

Chicken with Potatoes and Mushrooms

6 medium dried black Chinese mushrooms
1¼ pounds chicken thighs (about 5)
1 small egg
3 tablespoons rice wine
3 tablespoons soy sauce
1½ tablespoons cornstarch
3 tablespoons plus 1 teaspoon peanut oil
1 pound Idaho potatoes, pared (about 2)
3 green onions, white part only
1 tablespoon rice vinegar
1 teaspoon sugar
⅛ teaspoon pepper
4 cups vegetable oil
1 teaspoon minced pared fresh ginger root

1. Soften and clean mushrooms. Strain, cool and reserve ¼ cup soaking liquid.

2. Bone chicken thighs following directions in Steps 2 and 3 of "Chicken Stir-Fry with Radish" (see Index for page number); remove and discard skin if desired. Place

thighs skin-side-down; score diagonally in criss-cross pattern, cutting half-way through meat. Cut thighs lengthwise into ¾-inch wide strips; cut strips into ¾-inch squares.

3. Beat egg, 1 tablespoon rice wine and ½ tablespoon soy sauce in medium bowl; stir in chicken. Sprinkle with 1 tablespoon cornstarch; stir to mix well. Stir in 1 tablespoon peanut oil. Marinate at room temperature 30 minutes.

4. Cut potatoes into ¾-inch cubes; place in medium bowl

with cold water to cover. Slant-cut onions into ½-inch pieces. Cut mushrooms into ½-inch pieces.

5. Mix ½ tablespoon cornstarch with mushroom soaking liquid until smooth. Stir in 2½ tablespoons soy sauce, 2 tablespoons rice wine, the vinegar, sugar and pepper.

6. Heat wok over high heat 20 seconds; add vegetable oil and heat to 375°F. Drain potatoes; pat dry with paper toweling. Fry potatoes, ½ at a time, in hot oil until golden and partially cooked, 2 to 3

minutes. Remove potatoes with strainer; drain on paper toweling. Remove oil from wok; wipe clean.

7. Heat wok over high heat 15 seconds; add 2 tablespoons peanut oil and heat until hot, about 30 seconds. Reduce heat to medium; stir-fry onions and ginger 10 seconds. Increase heat to high. Scatter in chicken, ¼ at a time; stir-fry 1 minute after all chicken is added. Add potatoes and mushrooms; stir-fry 1 minute. Stir soy-sauce mixture; pour over chicken. Cook and stir until sauce thickens and coats ingredients, 30 to 45 seconds. Drizzle with 1 teaspoon peanut oil; stir 3 or 4 times. Serve immediately.

Makes 3 to 4 servings

50

Fish & Seafood

Velvet Shrimp

1 pound fresh small shrimp, shelled and deveined
2 tablespoons plus 2 teaspoons rice wine
2½ tablespoons cornstarch
1 large egg white
3½ tablespoons peanut oil
1 medium carrot, pared
1 cup boiling water
3 ounces Canadian bacon or ham
1 medium green bell pepper
1 small cucumber (about 6 inches long), pared
4 large dried black Chinese mushrooms, softened and cleaned
⅓ cup cold chicken stock or broth
2 tablespoons soy sauce
1 tablespoon rice vinegar
2 teaspoons sesame oil
1½ teaspoons sugar
2 cups vegetable oil
2 tablespoons finely chopped green onion, white part only
2 teaspoons minced pared fresh ginger root
½ cup frozen peas, thawed and drained

1. Combine shrimp and 2 teaspoons rice wine in medium bowl. Sprinkle with 2 tablespoons cornstarch; stir to mix well. Beat egg white very lightly in small bowl; stir into shrimp mixture. Stir in 1 tablespoon peanut oil; refrigerate, covered, 1 to 2 hours.

2. Cut carrot lengthwise in half; then cut crosswise into ³⁄₁₆-inch thick slices. Add carrot to boiling water in small saucepan; boil 1 minute. Rinse with cold water; drain well.

3. Cut bacon into ⅛-inch thick slices; cut the slices into ¾-inch diamond-shaped pieces. Cut green pepper into ¾-inch wide strips; cut strips diagonally into ¾-inch pieces. Cut cucumber lengthwise into quarters; scoop out and discard seeds. Cut cucumber diagonally into ½-inch slices. Cut mushrooms into quarters.

4. Mix ½ tablespoon cornstarch with chicken stock in small bowl until smooth; stir in 2 tablespoons rice wine, the soy sauce, rice vinegar, sesame oil and sugar.

5. Heat wok over high heat 20 seconds; add vegetable oil and heat over medium heat to 275°F. Velvet ⅓ of shrimp at a time: Stir shrimp; add to wok. Stir gently. Cook just until shrimp are pinkish-white outside but still raw in center, 20 to 30 seconds. Remove shrimp with strainer; drain on paper toweling. Reheat oil to 275°F and repeat with remaining shrimp. Remove oil from wok; wipe clean.

6. Heat wok over high heat 15 seconds; add 2 tablespoons peanut oil and heat until hot, about 30 seconds. Reduce heat to medium; stir-fry onion and ginger 10 seconds. Increase heat to high. Scatter in carrot and green pepper; stir-fry 30 seconds. Scatter in cucumber and mushrooms; stir-fry 30 seconds. Add bacon; stir-fry 30 seconds. Scatter in shrimp; stir-fry 30 seconds. Add peas; stir-fry 15 seconds. Stir stock mixture and add to wok; cook and stir until sauce thickens and coats ingredients, 15 to 20 seconds. Drizzle with ½ tablespoon peanut oil; stir 3 or 4 times. Serve immediately.
Makes 4 servings

Stir-Fried Squid Flowers

1 pound cleaned squid
3 thin slices fresh ginger root
3 tablespoons rice wine
3 teaspoons cornstarch
2 ounces canned bamboo
   shoots, rinsed and drained
1 small yellow onion
4 medium dried black
   Chinese mushrooms,
   softened and cleaned
3 ounces fresh snow peas
1 large carrot, pared
Boiling water
2 teaspoons cold water
¼ cup chicken stock or broth
¾ teaspoon sugar
½ teaspoon salt
¼ cup peanut oil
1 clove garlic, minced

1. Cut squid tentacles into 2 or 3 clusters. Pull back flaps off. Using scissors cut through thin line running lengthwise on bodies. Rinse bodies and flaps in cold water; pull off loose membranes. Drain well.

2. Lay bodies flat on cutting board, inside surface up. Hold cleaver at 45° angle to board; score lengthwise at ⅛-inch intervals, cutting ⅔ of the way through. Repeat on flaps.

3. Hold cleaver perpendicular to board. Score bodies crosswise at ⅛-inch intervals, cutting ½ way through squid on first 2 scorings; cut through every third scoring to make long thin strips. Cut strips crosswise into 1½- to 2-inch lengths. Rinse body pieces, flaps and tentacles in cold water; drain well.

4. Combine ginger with 1 tablespoon rice wine; stir in squid. Stir in 2 teaspoons cornstarch; mix well. Reserve at room temperature.

5. Cut bamboo shoots lengthwise into ⅛-inch thick slices; cut slices into 1¼ × ½-inch pieces. Cut onion lengthwise in half; cut halves lengthwise into ⅜-inch wide slices. Cut mushrooms into ½-inch wide strips.

6. Remove tips and strings from snow peas. Cut 5 or 6 evenly spaced wedges lengthwise from carrot; cut crosswise into ⅛-inch thick slices. Place snow peas in sieve; lower into saucepan of boiling water. Cook 15 seconds; remove. Rinse under cold water to cool. Drain well; transfer to plate. Repeat with carrot; cook 1 minute.

7. Mix 1 teaspoon cornstarch and the cold water until smooth. Add chicken stock, 2 tablespoons rice wine, the sugar and salt; stir until sugar dissolves.

8. Add squid to 2 quarts boiling water in wok; stir. Cook until pieces open and turn opaque white, about 45 seconds; remove with strainer. Drain on paper toweling. Discard ginger. Empty wok; wipe dry.

9. Heat wok over high heat 15 seconds; add oil and heat until hot, 30 seconds. Reduce heat to low; stir-fry garlic 10 seconds. Increase heat to high. Add onion; stir-fry 30 seconds. Add mushrooms; stir-fry 30 seconds. Add bamboo shoots, carrots, snow peas and squid, separately and in order; stir-fry 15 seconds after each addition.

10. Stir stock mixture; add to wok. Cook and stir until sauce thickens and coats ingredients, 20 seconds. Serve immediately.

Makes 3 to 4 servings

Flounder in Fresh Tomato Sauce

1 pound skinless flounder or
   sole fillets
3 tablespoons rice wine
1 teaspoon salt
⅛ teaspoon plus pinch white
   pepper
1 small egg white
2½ tablespoons cornstarch
4 tablespoons peanut oil
½ pound yellow onions
   (about 2 medium)
2 tablespoons cold water
¼ cup chicken stock or broth
½ pound fresh tomato (about
   1 large)
Boiling water
2 cups vegetable oil
⅓ cup catsup
½ cup frozen peas, thawed
   and drained

1. Cut fish into ¾-inch squares; combine with 1 tablespoon rice wine, ½ teaspoon salt and ⅛ teaspoon pepper. Beat egg white very lightly; stir into fish mixture to coat evenly. Stir in 1½ tablespoons

cornstarch; mix well. Stir in 1 tablespoon peanut oil; refrigerate, covered, 2 hours.

2. Cut onions crosswise into ¾-inch slices; cut slices into ¾-inch pieces. Mix 1 tablespoon cornstarch and the cold water in small bowl until smooth. Stir in chicken stock and 2 tablespoons rice wine.

3. Add tomato to small saucepan of boiling water; water should cover tomato. Cook 30 seconds. Remove tomato with slotted spoon; rinse under cold water to cool. Peel to-

mato; cut lengthwise into ¾-inch thick slices. Scoop out and discard seeds. Cut tomato slices into ¾-inch pieces.

4. Heat wok over high heat 20 seconds; add vegetable oil and heat over medium heat to 275°F. Velvet ½ of fish at a time: Stir fish; add to wok. Stir gently. Cook just until coating sets and fish turns white on outside, 30 to 45 seconds. Remove fish with strainer; drain on paper toweling. Reheat oil to 275°F and repeat with remaining fish. Remove oil from wok; wipe clean.

5. Heat wok over high heat 15 seconds; add 1 tablespoon peanut oil and heat until hot, about 30 seconds. Add onions; stir-fry until translucent, 2 minutes. Transfer to plate.

6. Add 2 tablespoons peanut oil to wok; heat until hot. Add tomato and catsup; stir-fry 1 minute. Add onions and peas; stir-fry 30 seconds. Stir cornstarch mixture; stir into wok. Add ½ teaspoon salt and the pinch pepper; cook and stir until sauce thickens, about 30 seconds. Add fish; cook and stir gently 30 seconds.

Makes 4 servings

Crispy Marinated Fish

1 whole fresh carp (2 to 2½ pounds), head and tail intact*
4 tablespoons soy sauce
2 tablespoons rice wine
3 medium dried black Chinese mushrooms, softened and cleaned
3 green onions, white part only
1 piece (3-inch) carrot, pared
½ ounce canned bamboo shoots, rinsed and drained
1 piece (1½ × ½ × ½-inch) fresh ginger root, pared
1 large clove garlic
¾ cup chicken stock or broth
3 tablespoons white vinegar
2 tablespoons catsup
2 tablespoons sugar
⅛ teaspoon pepper
¼ cup plus 2 teaspoons cornstarch
1½ tablespoons cold water
8 cups vegetable oil
3 tablespoons peanut oil
2 tablespoons frozen peas, thawed and drained

Other firm-fleshed fish such as striped bass can be used.

1. Score fish: Hold knife at 45° angle to board and on slight diagonal to fish; score both sides crosswise at 1-inch intervals, cutting to bone. Place fish in shallow glass bowl. Mix 2 tablespoons soy sauce and the rice wine; pour over fish and rub into all surfaces. Marinate at room temperature 20 minutes.

2. Cut mushrooms lengthwise into ⅛-inch wide strips. Cut onion lengthwise into ⅛-inch wide slivers. Cut carrot lengthwise into ⅛-inch thick slices; stack slices and cut lengthwise into ⅛-inch wide slivers. Repeat with bamboo shoots. Cut ginger lengthwise into 1/16-inch thick slices; stack slices and cut lengthwise into 1/16-inch wide slivers. Repeat with garlic.

3. Mix stock, vinegar, catsup, sugar, pepper and 2 tablespoons soy sauce; stir to dissolve sugar. Mix 2 teaspoons cornstarch and the cold water in a cup until smooth.

4. Heat wok over high heat 20 seconds; add vegetable oil and heat to 400°F. (Place wok securely in ring; oil will be deep when fish is added.) Remove fish from marinade; pat dry, including slits. Dust fish, including slits, with ¼ cup cornstarch; shake to remove excess. Hold fish by tail; slip head-first into oil. Fry until crispy, brown and cooked through, 8 to 10 minutes. Slip 2 slotted spatulas under fish and lift, draining excess oil; transfer fish to serving dish.

Remove vegetable oil from wok; wipe clean.

5. Heat wok over high heat 15 seconds; add peanut oil and heat until hot, 30 seconds. Add carrot and mushrooms; stir-fry 30 seconds. Add onions, bamboo shoots, ginger

and garlic; stir-fry 1 minute. Stir in stock mixture; heat to boiling. Stir in peas. Stir cornstarch mixture and add to wok; cook and stir until thickened, 30 seconds. Pour sauce over fish. Serve immediately.
Makes 3 to 4 servings

Butterflied Shrimp Stir-Fry

1 thin slice fresh ginger root
2½ tablespoons rice wine
¾ pound fresh medium shrimp, shelled and deveined
1 tablespoon cornstarch
1 small egg white
2 ounces canned bamboo shoots, rinsed and drained
2 ounces fresh snow peas
1 large stalk celery
4 medium dried black Chinese mushrooms, softened and cleaned
Boiling water
2 cups vegetable oil
2 tablespoons peanut oil
1 tablespoon chopped green onion, white part only
½ teaspoon minced pared fresh ginger root
¾ teaspoon sugar
½ teaspoon salt

1. Pare ginger root slice; pound lightly with flat side of cleaver. Combine with ½ tablespoon rice wine in medium bowl.

2. To butterfly shrimp: Cut lengthwise along outside curve, ¾ through body. Add shrimp to ginger and rice wine. Sprinkle with cornstarch; stir to mix well. Beat egg white very lightly in small bowl; stir into shrimp mixture. Refrigerate, covered, 1 to 2 hours.

3. Cut bamboo shoots lengthwise into ⅛-inch thick slices; cut slices into 2 × 1-inch pieces. Remove tips and strings from snow peas.

String celery; cut diagonally into ⅛-inch thick slices. Cut mushrooms in half.

4. Place snow peas in sieve; lower into medium saucepan of boiling water. Cook 15 seconds. Remove from water; rinse under cold running water to cool. Drain well; transfer to plate. Repeat process with celery, cooking 30 seconds.

5. Heat wok over high heat 20 seconds; add vegetable oil and heat over medium heat to 275°F. Remove and discard ginger from shrimp. Velvet ½ of shrimp at a time: Stir shrimp; add to wok. Stir gently to separate. Cook just until shrimp are pinkish white outside but still raw in center, 20 to 30 seconds. Remove shrimp with strainer; drain on paper toweling. Reheat oil to 275°F and repeat with remaining shrimp. Remove oil from wok; wipe clean.

6. Heat wok over high heat 15 seconds; add peanut oil and heat until hot, about 30 seconds. Reduce heat to medium; stir-fry mushrooms, onion and minced ginger 30 seconds. Increase heat to high. Add bamboo shoots; stir-fry 30 seconds. Add celery; stir-

fry 30 seconds. Add snow peas; stir-fry 15 seconds. Add shrimp; stir-fry 30 seconds. Add 2 tablespoons rice wine, the sugar and salt; cook and stir 15 seconds. Serve immediately.

Makes 3 servings

Squid Flowers with Spicy Dressing

1½ pounds cleaned squid
¾ pound celery hearts
Ice water
3½ tablespoons soy sauce
2½ tablespoons rice vinegar
2¼ teaspoons sugar
1½ teaspoons minced green onion, white part only
1½ teaspoons minced pared fresh ginger root
1 teaspoon sesame oil, if desired
½ to 1 teaspoon chili paste with garlic
2 quarts boiling water
1 sprig fresh parsley, if desired

1. Cut squid tentacle clusters into 2 or 3 small clusters. Pull back flaps off. Using scissors, cut through thin line running lengthwise on bodies. Rinse bodies and flaps in cold water; pull off loose membranes; drain well.

2. Lay bodies flat on cutting board, inside surface up. Hold cleaver at 45° angle to board; score lengthwise at ⅛-inch

intervals, cutting about ⅔ of the way through squid. Repeat on flaps.

3. Hold cleaver perpendicular to board. Score bodies crosswise at ⅛-inch intervals, cutting about ½ way through squid on first 2 scorings; cut

through every third scoring to make long thin strips. Rinse body strips, flaps and tentacles under cold water; drain.

4. Cut celery hearts into 3 × ⅛-inch sticks. Place in medium bowl of ice water; refrigerate. Combine soy sauce, vinegar, sugar, onion, ginger, sesame oil and chili paste in small bowl. Stir until sugar dissolves.

5. Add squid body strips to boiling water in wok; stir briskly to separate. Cook until strips open out and turn opaque white, about 45 seconds; remove with strainer. Drain on paper toweling. Repeat with back flaps and tentacles.

6. Drain celery well; arrange on serving plate. Place back flaps and tentacles in mound on top of celery. Arrange squid strips lengthwise on top of mound. Garnish with parsley. To serve, pour soy sauce dressing over squid and celery; toss lightly.

Makes 4 servings

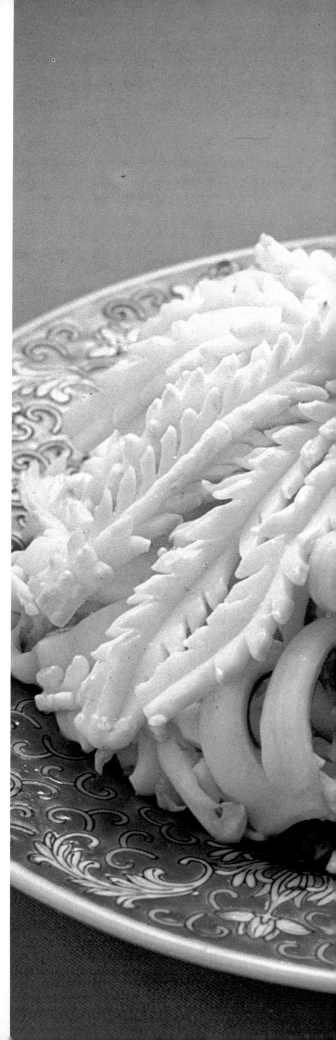

Imperial Prawns

¾ pound fresh prawns or large shrimp, in shells
1 can (10½ ounces) bamboo shoot tips, rinsed and drained
1 medium yellow onion
4 green onions, white part only
5 thin slices fresh ginger root
3 large dried black Chinese mushrooms, softened and cleaned
½ cup chicken stock or broth
1½ tablespoons rice wine
1 tablespoon sugar
2 to 3 teaspoons chili paste with garlic
1½ teaspoons soy sauce
Pinch pepper
5 tablespoons peanut oil
3 tablespoons catsup

1. Pull off and discard prawn legs; leave shells and tails intact, if desired. Cut through shell lengthwise on back of prawns with small scissors or sharp thin kife; devein prawns

leaving shells on. Slant-cut prawns into 1¼-inch pieces.

2. Roll-cut bamboo shoots into ¾-inch pieces. Cut yellow onion crosswise in half;

cut each half lengthwise into ½-inch wedges. Slant-cut green onions into ¾-inch pieces. Pare ginger root; cut into small squares. Cut mushrooms into quarters.

3. Mix stock, rice wine, sugar, chili paste, soy sauce and pepper in small bowl.

4. Heat wok over high heat 15 seconds; add 3 tablespoons oil and heat until hot, about 30 seconds. Scatter in prawns, ¼ at a time; stir-fry just until opaque, 1 to 1½ minutes after all prawns are added. Turn off heat; remove prawns with slotted spoon to plate.

5. Add 1 tablespoon oil to wok; heat over high heat until hot. Reduce heat to medium; stir-fry green onions and ginger 10 seconds. Increase heat to high; scatter in bam-

boo shoots, yellow onion and mushrooms. Stir-fry until yellow onion begins to wilt, about 2 minutes. Add catsup; stir-fry 10 seconds. Stir in stock mixture; cook and stir until liquid is reduced to a medium coating consistency, 2 to 3 minutes. Return prawns to wok; cook and stir 15 sec-

onds. Drizzle with 1 tablespoon oil; stir 3 or 4 times. Serve immediately.

Makes 3 servings

Mackerel with Black Bean Sauce

1 can (15 ounces) mackerel in water, drained well
2 tablespoons fermented black beans
3 tablespoons chicken stock or broth
1 tablespoon soy sauce
1 tablespoon rice wine
½ teaspoon sugar
Pinch pepper
2 tablespoons peanut oil
1 tablespoon minced pared fresh ginger root
1 large clove garlic, minced
3 tablespoons minced green onion, white part only
1½ teaspoons rice vinegar
1 tablespoon minced fresh parsley

1. Carefully remove mackerel from can to plate. Remove skin and bones if desired; leave mackerel in as large pieces as possible.

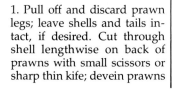

2. Place black beans in sieve; rinse under cold running water a few seconds to remove excess salt. Drain well on paper toweling.

3. Mix chicken stock, soy sauce, rice wine, sugar and pepper in small bowl.

4. Heat wok over high heat 15 seconds; add oil and heat until hot, about 30 seconds. Add beans, ginger and garlic; stir-fry 15 seconds. Reduce heat to low. Add stock mixture and onion; cook and stir 30 seconds.

5. Increase heat to medium. Add mackerel to wok. Cook and stir gently until mackerel is heated through and evenly coated with seasonings. Drizzle with vinegar; stir 2 or 3 times. Transfer to heated serving dish; sprinkle with parsley. Serve immediately.

Makes 3 servings

Braised Belt Fish

3 thin slices fresh ginger root
1 green onion
⅓ cup plus 1½ tablespoons rice wine
¼ cup plus 2 teaspoons soy sauce
2 pounds belt fish, thawed*
⅓ cup distilled white vinegar
¼ cup sugar
⅓ cup plus 3 tablespoons peanut oil
Fresh parsley sprigs, if desired

Belt fish, a long thin scaleless fish with thin silvery skin, is available frozen in many Oriental grocery stores. If unavailable, substitute any long thin firm-fleshed fish.

1. Pare ginger root. Pound ginger and onion lightly with flat side of cleaver. Cut onion into 1-inch lengths. Combine ginger, onion, 1½ tablespoons rice wine and 2 teaspoons soy sauce in glass bowl.

2. Cut off and discard head and tail of fish; cut crosswise into 4-inch long pieces. Score both sides of fish lengthwise at ½-inch intervals, making cuts ⅛-inch deep.

3. Place fish in glass bowl with ginger marinade; rub all surfaces with marinade. Marinate at room temperature 10 to 15 minutes.

4. Combine vinegar, sugar, ⅓ cup rice wine, and ¼ cup soy sauce in small bowl. Stir until sugar is dissolved. Remove fish from marinade; pat dry.

5. Heat wok over high heat 30 seconds; add ⅓ cup oil and heat until hot, about 1 minute. Arrange fish in wok in single layer. Fry, turning fish once, until brown, 1½ to 2 minutes per side. Tilt wok occasionally to spread oil. Transfer fish to plate. Discard oil; wipe wok clean.

6. Heat wok over high heat 15 seconds; add 3 tablespoons oil and heat until hot, about 30 seconds. Add vinegar mixture; heat to boiling. Return fish to wok in single layer;

heat until liquid returns to boiling. Reduce heat to low. Simmer uncovered, turning fish once, 3 minutes per side. Remove fish to heated serving dish; pull off and discard back fin.

7. Heat liquid in wok over high heat to boiling. Boil and stir vigorously for 1 minute. Strain sauce. Pour about ½ sauce over fish. Garnish with parsley. Serve immediately. Serve remaining sauce in separate small bowl.

Makes 4 servings

Creamy Squid

1 pound cleaned squid
3 tablespoons rice wine
¾ teaspoon salt
2 tablespoons plus ½ teaspoon cornstarch
1 medium cucumber, pared
3 green onions, white part only
3 medium dried black Chinese mushrooms, softened and cleaned
1½ tablespoons cold water
½ cup chicken stock or broth
1 teaspoon sugar
Pinch white pepper
2 cups vegetable oil
2 tablespoons peanut oil
1 teaspoon minced pared fresh ginger root
¼ cup whipping cream

1. Cut squid tentacle clusters into 3 small clusters. Pull back flaps off. Using scissors, cut through thin line running lengthwise on bodies. Rinse bodies and flaps in cold water; pull off loose membranes. Drain well.

2. Lay bodies flat on cutting board, inside surface up. Hold cleaver at 45° angle to board; score lengthwise at ⅛-inch intervals, cutting about ⅔ of the way through squid. Repeat on flaps.

3. Cut bodies lengthwise into 1½ to 2-inch wide strips; cut strips crosswise into ⅜-inch wide pieces. Rinse pieces, flaps and tentacles under cold running water. Drain well; pat dry with paper toweling.

4. Combine 1½ tablespoons rice wine and ½ teaspoon salt; stir in squid. Stir in 1½ tablespoons cornstarch; mix well. Marinate at room temperature 20 minutes.

5. Cut cucumber lengthwise in half; scoop out and discard seeds. Cut each half lengthwise into ⅜-inch wide strips; cut strips crosswise into 2-inch lengths. Slant-cut onions into ¼-inch slices. Cut mushrooms into ¼-inch wide strips.

6. Mix 2 teaspoons cornstarch and the cold water until smooth. Add chicken stock, sugar, pepper, 1½ tablespoons rice wine and ¼ teaspoon salt; stir to dissolve sugar.

7. Heat wok over high heat 20 seconds; add vegetable oil and heat over medium heat to 275°F. Stir squid. Velvet ½ of squid at a time: Add squid to wok; stir gently. Cook just until pieces curl and turn opaque white, 1 minute. Remove with strainer; drain on paper toweling. Reheat oil to 275°F; repeat with remaining squid. Remove oil and wipe wok clean.

8. Heat wok over high heat 15 seconds. Add peanut oil; heat until hot, 30 seconds. Scatter in cucumbers and mushrooms; stir-fry 1½ minutes. Reduce heat to medium. Add onions and ginger; stir-fry 10 seconds. Add squid; stir-fry 10 seconds. Stir stock mixture and add to wok; increase heat to high. Cook and stir until thickened, 45 seconds; turn off heat. Add cream; stir well.

Makes 3 to 4 servings

Batter-Fried Shrimp

¾ pound fresh medium
 shrimp, shelled and
 deveined
2 teaspoons rice wine
¼ cup plus 1½ tablespoons
 cornstarch
Sweet and Sour Dipping
 Sauce (recipe follows)
1 small cucumber (for
 garnish)
⅓ cup cold water
2 large eggs, separated
¾ cup all-purpose flour
2 teaspoons baking powder
2 tablespoons lard, melted
¼ teaspoon salt
4 cups vegetable oil

1. Combine shrimp and rice
wine in medium bowl.
Sprinkle with 1½ tablespoons

cornstarch; stir to mix well.
Marinate at room temperature
30 minutes.

2. Prepare Sweet and Sour
Dipping Sauce.

3. For garnish: Cut cucumber
lengthwise in half; cut halves
lengthwise into ⅜-inch wide
strips. Lay strips on sides; cut
off seeds leaving ⅜-inch
cucumber attached to skin.
Cut strips crosswise into 3-
inch pieces. Starting ½ inch
from one end of each piece,
cut lengthwise into 5 equally
spaced slices. Leave center
slice upright; fold outer slices
inward and tuck in at base to
form petals. Refrigerate covered.

4. Mix ¼ cup cornstarch with
the water in a cup until
smooth. Beat egg whites in
small bowl until stiff but not
dry. Beat egg yolks in medium
bowl; stir in cornstarch mixture. Whisk in flour until
smooth. Fold in egg whites
with whisk until smooth. Stir

in baking powder; let batter
stand until bubbly, about 5
minutes. Stir in lard and salt.

5. Heat wok over high heat 20
seconds; add oil and heat to
325°F. Using ⅓ of shrimp at a
time, dip each shrimp into
batter and add to wok. Fry,

stirring gently and turning occasionally, until golden and
cooked through, 3 to 4 minutes. Remove shrimp with
strainer; drain on wire rack
lined with paper toweling.
Reheat oil to 325°F and repeat
with remaining shrimp.

6. Heat oil to 350°F. Fry
shrimp again, about ½ at a
time (do not dip in batter
again), until deep golden and
crisp, 2 to 3 minutes. Remove
with strainer; drain on wire
rack lined with paper toweling. Arrange shrimp on serving plate with cucumber garnish. Serve immediately with
Sweet and Sour Dipping
Sauce.

Makes 3 to 4 servings

Sweet and Sour Dipping Sauce

2 tablespoons sugar
2 teaspoons cornstarch
¼ teaspoon salt
⅓ cup catsup
2 tablespoons distilled white
 vinegar
1 tablespoon rice wine
1 tablespoon soy sauce

1. Mix sugar, cornstarch and
salt in small saucepan until
well blended. Stir in remaining ingredients until smooth.

2. Heat the mixture over medium-high heat to boiling; reduce heat to low. Cook and
stir until sauce thickens and
bubbles for 2 minutes. Transfer to small bowl; cover surface of sauce with plastic
wrap. Sauce can be refrigerated up to 3 days. Serve warm
or at room temperature.

Makes about ½ cup

Roasted Pepper-Salt

2 tablespoons Szechuan
 peppercorns
⅔ cup coarse (Kosher) salt

1. Scatter peppercorns in
small, heavy, dry skillet. Pour
salt over peppercorns. Heat,
uncovered, over medium-low
heat, stirring occasionally,
until salt begins to color and
pepper is fragrant, 5 to 8 minutes. Pepper will smoke;
lower heat if needed to prevent burning.

2. Transfer mixture to mortar
or small bowl; crush with pestle or handle of cleaver. Strain
mixture through sieve to remove peppercorn husks; cool.
Store in airtight container in
cool dry place. Pepper-salt
will keep for several months.

Makes about ⅔ cup

Sweet and Sour Flounder

1 pound skinless flounder, haddock or cod fillets
2 tablespoons rice wine
½ teaspoon salt
2 pinches white pepper
¼ cup plus 2½ teaspoons cornstarch
¼ cup plus 1½ tablespoons cold water
⅓ cup chicken stock or broth
3 tablespoons sugar
1 tablespoon soy sauce
1 tablespoon catsup
1 large egg
⅓ cup all-purpose flour
4 cups vegetable oil
2 tablespoons peanut oil
¼ cup chopped green onion, white part only
1 tablespoon minced pared fresh ginger root
½ teaspoon minced garlic
3 tablespoons distilled white vinegar

1. If using flounder or haddock, cut into 1½×1-inch pieces; if using cod, cut into 1-inch squares. Combine in medium bowl with rice wine, ¼ teaspoon salt and pinch pepper.

2. Mix 2½ teaspoons cornstarch and 1½ tablespoons cold water in small bowl until smooth. Add stock, sugar, soy sauce and catsup; stir until sugar dissolves.

3. Mix ¼ cup cornstarch and ¼ cup cold water in small bowl until smooth. Whisk in egg. Add flour, ¼ teaspoon salt and pinch pepper; whisk until smooth. Reserve batter.

4. Heat wok over high heat 20 seconds; add vegetable oil and heat to 350°F. Drain fish; pat dry with paper toweling. Add ½ the fish pieces to batter; stir to coat well. Remove from batter, one piece at a time, and add to wok. Fry over medium-high heat, stirring gently occasionally, until crisp, golden and fish is cooked through, 3 to 4 minutes. Remove fish with strainer; drain on paper toweling. Repeat with remaining fish. Arrange fish on serving dish. Remove oil from wok; wipe clean.

5. Heat wok over high heat 15 seconds; add peanut oil and heat until hot, about 30 seconds. Reduce heat to medium. Add onion, ginger and garlic; stir-fry 10 seconds. Increase heat to high. Stir stock mixture; add to wok. Cook and stir until sauce thickens and bubbles, about 1 minute. Stir in vinegar; cook 10 seconds. Pour over fish.

Makes 4 servings

Spicy Shrimp with Peas

1 pound fresh very small shrimp, shelled and deveined*
2 tablespoons plus 2 teaspoons rice wine
3 tablespoons cornstarch
1 large egg white
4 tablespoons peanut oil
⅓ cup catsup
1 tablespoon soy sauce
½ cup cold water
2 cups vegetable oil
2 tablespoons minced pared fresh ginger root
1 to 2 teaspoons minced garlic
1 to 2 teaspoons chili sauce
1 tablespoon sugar
¼ teaspoon salt
½ cup frozen peas, thawed
⅓ cup finely chopped green onions, white part only
2 teaspoons rice vinegar

If very small shrimp are unavailable, cut shrimp crosswise into 1-inch lengths after cleaning.

1. Combine shrimp and 2 teaspoons rice wine in medium bowl. Sprinkle with 2 tablespoons cornstarch; stir to mix well. Beat egg white very lightly in small bowl; stir into shrimp mixture. Stir in 1 tablespoon peanut oil; refrigerate, covered, 1 to 2 hours.

2. Mix catsup, 2 tablespoons rice wine and the soy sauce in small bowl. Mix 1 tablespoon cornstarch and the cold water in a cup until smooth.

3. Heat wok over high heat 20 seconds; add vegetable oil and heat over medium heat to 275°F. Velvet ⅓ of shrimp at a time: Stir shrimp; add to wok. Stir gently to separate. Cook just until shrimp are pinkish white outside but still raw in

center, 20 to 30 seconds. Remove shrimp with strainer; drain on paper toweling. Reheat oil to 275°F and repeat with remaining shrimp. Remove oil from wok; wipe clean.

4. Heat wok over high heat 15 seconds; add 2 tablespoons peanut oil and heat until hot, about 30 seconds. Reduce heat to medium; stir-fry ginger and garlic 15 seconds. Stir in chili sauce; stir-fry 5 seconds. Increase heat to high. Stir in catsup mixture, the sugar and salt; cook and stir 15 seconds.

5. Add peas, shrimp and onions to wok; cook and stir 30 seconds. Stir cornstarch mixture and add to wok, pouring it around edge of liquid in wok. Cook, stir and fold mixture until sauce thickens and coats shrimp evenly, 30 to 45 seconds. Drizzle with vinegar and 1 tablespoon peanut oil; stir 3 or 4 times. Serve immediately.

Makes 4 servings

Fried Fish with Pepper Sauce

8 whole fresh small mackerel (about 8 ounces each) heads and tails intact
5 tablespoons minced green onion, white part only
4 tablespoons rice wine
4 teaspoons minced pared fresh ginger root
1 large egg white
2½ tablespoons cold water
½ teaspoon salt
⅛ teaspoon black pepper
1 cup plus 1 tablespoon cornstarch
1 to 2 dried red chili peppers, seeded
½ cup chicken stock or broth
2 tablespoons soy sauce
1½ tablespoons distilled white vinegar
1½ tablespoons sugar
1 teaspoon minced garlic
8 cups vegetable oil
3 tablespoons peanut oil

1. Cut small fish: Hold cleaver perpendicular to fish; cut crosswise in center just to bone. Turn cleaver almost parallel to fish; slice along bone up to gills to make flap. Repeat process to make second flap starting at tail and ending ½-inch from center of fish. Turn fish over; cut 2 flaps.

2. Combine 1 tablespoon onion, 2 tablespoons rice wine and 1 teaspoon ginger. Rub on fish, including insides of flaps. Reserve at room temperature.

3. For batter, lightly whisk egg white; whisk in 1 tablespoon cold water, the salt and pepper. Add ½ cup cornstarch; whisk until smooth.

4. Cut chili pepper into ⅛-inch pieces. Mix 1 tablespoon cornstarch and 1½ tablespoons cold water in small bowl until smooth; stir in stock, soy sauce, vinegar, sugar, garlic, ¼ cup onion, 2 tablespoons rice wine and 1 tablespoon ginger. Spread ½ cup cornstarch on plate.

5. Pat fish dry with paper toweling. Rub inside flaps with thin layer of batter; dust with cornstarch. Close flaps. Rub outside of fish with thin layer of batter; coat with cornstarch. Hold tail; shake to remove excess cornstarch.

6. Heat wok over high heat 20 seconds; add vegetable oil and heat to 350°F. (Place wok securely in ring; oil will be deep when fish are added.) Fry ½ of fish: Hold fish by head and slide tail-first into wok; fry 2 minutes. Remove with strainer; drain on paper toweling. Reheat oil to 350°F; fry remaining ½ fish for 2 min-

utes. Return all fish to wok; fry until cooked through and crisp, 3 to 4 minutes. Remove fish from wok; drain well. Arrange on serving dish. Empty wok; wipe clean.

7. Heat wok over high heat 15 seconds; add peanut oil and heat until hot, 30 seconds. Reduce heat to medium; add chili peppers and stir-fry until dark red, 10 seconds. Stir stock mixture; add to wok. Increase heat to high; cook and stir until sauce thickens, 1 minute. Pour over fish.

Makes 4 servings

Squid with Cucumbers and Mushrooms

1 pound cleaned squid
3 thin slices fresh ginger root
4½ tablespoons rice wine
1 teaspoon salt
2 tablespoons cornstarch
1 medium cucumber, pared
6 ounces fresh or canned button mushrooms
1 tablespoon cold water
¼ cup chicken stock or broth
1½ teaspoons rice vinegar
1½ teaspoons sugar
Pinch white pepper
3 tablespoons minced green onion, white part only
1 tablespoon minced pared fresh ginger root
2 cups vegetable oil
4 tablespoons peanut oil

1. Cut squid tentacles into 4 clusters. Pull flaps off. Using scissors, cut through thin line running lengthwise on bodies. Rinse bodies and flaps in cold water; pull off loose membranes. Drain well.

2. Lay bodies flat on cutting board, inside surface up. Hold cleaver perpendicular to board; score lengthwise at ⅛-inch intervals, cutting about ¾ of the way through squid. Repeat on flaps.

3. Turn bodies and flaps over, scored-side-down. Cut crosswise (at right angle to scoring) into ¾-inch wide strips. Cut strips crosswise into ¾-inch pieces. Rinse pieces and tentacles under cold water. Drain well; pat dry with paper toweling.

4. Place ginger slices, 1½ tablespoons rice wine and ½ teaspoon salt in medium bowl. Stir in squid. Stir in 1½ tablespoons cornstarch; mix well. Marinate at room temperature 20 minutes.

5. Cut cucumber lengthwise in half; scoop out and discard seeds. Cut each half lengthwise into 6 strips; cut strips diagonally into ⅜-inch wide slices. Cut mushrooms in half.

6. Mix ½ tablespoon cornstarch and the cold water until smooth. Add stock, vinegar, sugar, pepper, 3 tablespoons rice wine and ½ teaspoon salt; stir to dissolve sugar. Stir in onion and minced ginger.

7. Heat wok over high heat 20 seconds, add vegetable oil and heat over medium heat to 275°F. Stir squid; discard ginger. Velvet ½ of squid at a time: Add squid to wok; stir gently. Cook until pieces curl and turn opaque white, about 1 minute. Remove with strainer; drain on paper toweling. Reheat oil to 275°F and

repeat with remaining squid. Remove oil; wipe wok clean.

8. Heat wok over high heat 15 seconds. Add 3 tablespoons peanut oil and heat until hot, about 30 seconds. Scatter in mushrooms; stir-fry 30 seconds. Scatter in cucumber; stir-fry until cucumber turns bright green, 1 to 1½ minutes. Scatter in squid; stir-fry 10 seconds. Stir stock mixture; add to wok. Cook and stir until sauce thickens, 1 minute. Drizzle with 1 tablespoon peanut oil; stir 3 or 4 times.

Makes 3 to 4 servings

Eggs & Bean Curd

Dow Foo Custard

6 ounces bean curd, rinsed
¾ cup plus ⅓ cup chicken
   stock or broth
8 ounces fresh shimeiji
   mushrooms (or 15-ounce
   can straw mushrooms,
   rinsed and drained)
4 or 5 round slices Canadian
   bacon or ham (3 to 4
   ounces)
4 large egg whites
½ cup milk
1¼ teaspoons salt
⅛ teaspoon white pepper
Boiling water
2 tablespoons peanut oil
¾ cup fresh broccoli
   flowerets
¼ cup plus 2 teaspoons cold
   water
1 teaspoon cornstarch

1. Crumble bean curd coarsely; press between several layers of paper toweling to remove excess moisture. Combine bean curd and ⅓ cup stock in blender container; puree until smooth.

2. Trim root ends of mushrooms; break into small clusters. Arrange mushrooms in a border near edge of heatproof dish about 9 inches in diameter and 1 inch deep. Cut bacon slices crosswise in half; arrange upright and overlapping in a circle inside the mushroom border.

3. Beat egg whites very lightly in medium bowl; gently whisk in bean curd mixture until smooth. Add milk, ¾ teaspoon salt and the pepper; stir with whisk until thoroughly mixed.

4. Pour bean curd mixture into center of prepared dish. Use as much of the custard as will fit without flowing over ham slices. Place dish in steamer. Spread clean thin kitchen towel over steamer; cover with lid.

5. Place steamer in wok; add boiling water to wok to level of 1 inch below steamer. Adjust heat for gentle steady steam, about medium. Steam custard just until knife inserted in center is withdrawn clean, about 10 minutes. Remove steamer from wok; empty wok and wipe dry.

6. Heat wok over high heat 15 seconds; add oil and heat until hot, about 30 seconds. Add broccoli; stir-fry 1 minute. Add ¼ cup water; cover and steam-cook until crisp-tender, about 30 seconds. Remove broccoli; drain on paper toweling. Dry wok.

7. Heat ¾ cup stock and ½ teaspoon salt in wok over high heat to boiling; reduce heat to medium. Mix cornstarch and 2 teaspoons cold water in a cup until smooth; add to wok. Cook and stir until sauce thickens, about 1 minute.

8. Remove dish from steamer; blot water around edge of dish with paper toweling. Arrange broccoli in center of custard.

9. Gently ladle about ½ of sauce over custard to cover with a thin film. Serve custard immediately with remaining sauce, if desired.
Makes 4 servings

Simmered Pork and Bean Curd Balls

½ pound bean curd, rinsed and drained
½ pound ground pork, march-chopped
1 large egg, lightly beaten
3 tablespoons rice wine
1½ tablespoons plus 1 teaspoon soy sauce
1¼ teaspoons sugar
1 teaspoon sesame oil
¼ teaspoon salt
Pinch pepper
3½ tablespoons cornstarch
⅛ ounce dried cloud ears, softened and cleaned
6 leaves napa or celery cabbage
2 green onions, white part only
1½ cups chicken stock or broth
2 tablespoons cold water
3 cups vegetable oil
1½ tablespoons peanut oil
2 teaspoons minced pared fresh ginger root
½ star anise

1. Coarsely crumble bean curd and spread on several layers of paper toweling; drain 10 minutes. Blot firmly with additional paper toweling.

2. Combine bean curd and pork in large bowl; mix with hand until mixture is of uniform color and texture. Add egg, 2 tablespoons rice wine, 1 teaspoon soy sauce, ½ teaspoon sugar, the sesame oil, salt and pepper; mix thoroughly. Sprinkle with 2½ tablespoons cornstarch; mix thoroughly. Shape into 1-inch balls; mixture will be soft but

will hold its shape. Reserve meatballs in single layer, uncovered, at room temperature.

3. Break cloud ears into 1½-inch pieces. Cut napa leaves lengthwise in half; slant-cut into 1½-inch pieces. Cut onions into ½-inch pieces. Mix chicken stock, 1½ tablespoons soy sauce, 1 tablespoon rice wine and ¾ teaspoon sugar in small bowl. Mix 1 tablespoon cornstarch and the cold water in a cup until smooth.

4. Heat wok over high heat 20 seconds; add vegetable oil and heat to 375°F. Fry meatballs,

⅓ at a time, stirring gently, until light brown, about 1 minute. Remove with strainer; drain on paper toweling. Reheat oil to 375°F and repeat with remaining meatballs. Remove oil from wok; wipe clean.

5. Heat wok over high heat 15 seconds; add 1 tablespoon peanut oil and heat until hot, about 30 seconds. Scatter in napa; stir-fry 15 seconds. Add stock mixture; stir in meatballs, onions, ginger and star anise. Heat to boiling; reduce heat to maintain simmer. Simmer meatballs, covered, until cooked through, 15 minutes. Uncover and cook over medium heat to reduce liquid slightly, about 5 minutes. Add cloud ears. Stir cornstarch mixture; add to wok. Cook and stir gently until sauce is thickened, about 30 seconds. Drizzle with ½ tablespoon peanut oil; stir 3 or 4 times. Serve immediately.
Makes 3 to 4 servings

Ginger Crab and Eggs

4 ounces fresh or thawed frozen crab meat
1 tablespoon rice wine
4 large green onions, white part only
2½ ounces canned bamboo shoots, rinsed and drained
4 thin slices fresh ginger root
4 large eggs
½ teaspoon salt
⅛ teaspoon white pepper
¼ cup peanut oil

1. Break crab meat into coarse shreds with fingers, picking out any bits of shell or cartilage. Combine crab with ½ tablespoon rice wine in small bowl. Marinate at room temperature 15 minutes.

2. Cut onions lengthwise in half; place cut-side-down on cutting board. Pound onions lightly with flat side of cleaver; spread as flat as possible. Cut on a sharp diagonal into 1/16-inch shreds.

3. Cut bamboo shoots into 1/16-inch thick slices; cut slices into 2×⅛-inch shreds. Pare ginger root; cut into very fine shreds. Beat eggs in medium bowl with salt and pepper.

4. Heat wok over high heat 15 seconds; add oil and heat until hot, about 30 seconds. Add bamboo shoots, onions and ginger; stir-fry 15 seconds. Add crab; stir-fry 15 seconds. Stir in ½ tablespoon rice wine; cook and stir 5 seconds.

5. Stir eggs into wok; cook undisturbed a few seconds. As eggs begin to cook on bottom and puff at edges, push cooked portion to one side, tilting wok in opposite direction, letting uncooked portion flow down; repeat until eggs are ¾ cooked, about 15 seconds in all. Stir with quick light motion to break up eggs slightly and complete cooking. Serve immediately.
Makes 3 servings

Ma-Po Bean Curd

1 pound bean curd
6 ounces boneless pork
  shoulder
4 green onions, white part
  only
1 large green bell pepper
4 medium dried black
  Chinese mushrooms,
  softened and cleaned
1 cup chicken stock or broth
2 tablespoons soy sauce
1 tablespoon rice wine
½ teaspoon sugar
1 tablespoon cornstarch
2 tablespoons cold water
3 cups vegetable oil
4 tablespoons peanut oil
1 tablespoon minced pared
  fresh ginger root
1 large clove garlic, minced
1 tablespoon ground brown
  bean sauce
¼ teaspoon cayenne pepper

1. Cut bean curd into ¼-inch thick slices. Drain on layers of paper toweling. Cut slices in half diagonally to form triangles. Press with dry paper toweling to remove moisture; repeat several times.

2. Cut pork across the grain into ⅛-inch thick slices; cut slices into 2×1-inch pieces. Cut onions into 1¼-inch

lengths. Cut green pepper lengthwise into 1-inch wide strips; cut each strip diagonally in half lengthwise to form triangles. Cut mushrooms in half.

3. Mix stock, soy sauce, rice wine and sugar in small bowl. Mix cornstarch and cold water in a cup until smooth.

4. Heat wok over high heat 20 seconds; add vegetable oil and heat to 375°F. Reduce heat to medium. Slip as many bean curd pieces into wok as will fit in single layer. Fry, stirring gently and turning occasionally, until pale golden and slightly crisp, about 3 minutes. Remove with strainer; drain on paper toweling. Reheat oil to 375°F and repeat with remaining bean curd. Remove oil; wipe wok clean.

5. Heat wok over high heat 15 seconds; add 2 tablespoons peanut oil and heat until hot, about 30 seconds. Add green pepper, onions and mushrooms to wok; stir-fry 1 minute. Remove to plate.

6. Add 2 tablespoons peanut oil to wok; heat until hot. Reduce heat to medium; stir-fry ginger and garlic 10 seconds. Increase heat to high; scatter in pork ½ at a time, and stir-fry until no longer pink, 1 to 1½ minutes after all pork is added. Stir in bean sauce and cayenne pepper; stir-fry 5 seconds. Return green pepper mixture to wok; stir-fry 15 seconds. Stir in bean curd and stock mixture. Heat to simmering; reduce heat to low. Simmer, uncovered, 2 minutes. Stir cornstarch mixture and add to wok; cook and stir until sauce is thickened, about 30 seconds.

Makes 3 to 4 servings

Egg Custard with Meat Sauce

3½ tablespoons peanut oil
2 large dried black Chinese
  mushrooms, softened and
  cleaned
2 ounces canned bamboo
  shoots, rinsed and drained
3 cups chicken stock or broth,
  at room temperature
4 tablespoons rice wine
3 tablespoons soy sauce
1 tablespoon Chinese black
  vinegar
2 teaspoons sugar
1½ tablespoons cornstarch
3 tablespoons cold water
5 large eggs, at room
  temperature
¾ teaspoon salt
Pinch white pepper
Boiling water
6 ounces ground pork or beef,
  march-chopped
2 tablespoons chopped green
  onion, white part only
2 teaspoons minced pared
  fresh ginger root
½ to 1 teaspoon chili paste
  with garlic

1. Rub inside of heatproof 2-quart shallow bowl (which

fits into steamer basket) with ½ tablespoon oil.

2. Dice mushrooms and bamboo shoots into ⅛-inch cubes. Mix 1¼ cups stock, 2 tablespoons rice wine, the soy sauce, vinegar and sugar in small bowl. Mix cornstarch and cold water until smooth.

3. Beat eggs in medium bowl just until thoroughly combined. Gently and gradually stir in 1¾ cups stock; stir in 2 tablespoons rice wine, the salt and pepper. Pour into oiled bowl; cover bowl with foil. Place bowl in steamer; cover

steamer. Place in wok; add boiling water to wok to level of 1 inch below steamer. Adjust heat for gentle steady steam, about medium.

4. Steam custard just until knife inserted in center is withdrawn clean, 15 to 20 minutes. Remove steamer from wok; uncover custard. Empty wok and wipe dry.

5. Heat wok over high heat 15 seconds; add 2 tablespoons oil and heat until hot, about 30 seconds. Add pork; stir-fry until pork changes color,

about 1 minute. Add bamboo shoots and mushrooms; stir-fry 30 seconds. Add onion, ginger and chili paste; stir-fry 10 seconds. Stir in soy-sauce mixture; heat to boiling. Stir in cornstarch mixture; cook and stir until sauce thickens, about 45 seconds. Drizzle with 1 tablespoon oil; stir 3 or 4 times. Turn off heat.

6. Remove custard bowl from steamer. Gently ladle pork mixture over custard. Serve immediately.

Makes 4 to 6 servings

Chrysanthemum with Eggs and Ham

3 tablespoons plus 1 teaspoon
    peanut oil
1½ tablespoons white sesame
    seeds
2 ounces sliced ham
3 medium dried black
    Chinese mushrooms,
    softened and cleaned
4 large eggs
¼ teaspoon salt
1 bunch (about 12 ounces)
    edible chrysanthemum*
3 quarts boiling water
2 tablespoons plus 1 teaspoon
    soy sauce
1½ teaspoons sugar
1 teaspoon sesame oil

*Edible chrysanthemum is available in spring and summer in Oriental grocery stores. Broccoli can be substituted. Omit Step 3. Cut broccoli flowerets into 1-inch pieces. Pare stalks; cut into 1½×⅜×⅜-inch pieces. Stir-fry in 3 tablespoons peanut oil 1 minute; add ⅓ cup water and cook covered, until crisp-tender, 45 seconds. Drain; place in medium bowl.

1. Heat wok over high heat 15 seconds; add 1 teaspoon peanut oil and heat 15 seconds. Wipe out; leave thin oil coating. Reduce heat to medium. Add sesame seeds to wok; cook and stir until light brown, 30 to 45 seconds. Transfer to plate; cool.

2. Cut ham into ½-inch squares. Cut mushrooms into ⅜-inch pieces. Beat eggs with salt.

3. Rinse chrysanthemum in cold water; drain. Cut off and discard yellowed leaves and tough portion of stems. Add chrysanthemum to boiling water in large saucepan. Cook over high heat just until leaves are wilted and stems are crisp-tender, 1½ to 2 minutes; drain immediately. Rinse under cold running water just until cool enough to handle;

drain well. Arrange chrysanthemum lengthwise in a pile, cut crosswise into 1½-inch lengths. Place in medium bowl.

4. Crush sesame seeds in mortar with pestle or in small bowl with cleaver handle to

coarse powder. Combine crushed seeds, 2 tablespoons soy sauce, the sugar and sesame oil in small bowl; stir to mix well. Pour over chrysanthemum; toss to mix. Arrange on serving dish.

5. Heat wok over high heat 15 seconds; add ½ tablespoon peanut oil and heat until hot, about 30 seconds. Reduce heat to medium. Add mushrooms; stir-fry 45 seconds. Drizzle with 1 teaspoon soy sauce; stir to mix. Transfer to plate; wipe wok clean.

6. Add ½ tablespoon peanut oil to wok; heat over high heat until hot. Add ham; stir-fry until heated through, 30 seconds. Transfer to plate.

7. Add 2 tablespoons peanut oil to wok; heat until hot. Add eggs, quickly swirl around wok. As eggs begin to puff at edges, push cooked portion to one side, tilting wok in opposite direction, letting uncooked portion flow down. When eggs are about ¾ set, begin chopping into small pieces with spatula. (Work quickly; total cooking time for eggs is about 20 seconds.) Arrange eggs on chrysanthemum. Top with ham, then with mushrooms. Serve immediately.

Makes 3 to 4 servings

Stir-Fried Eggs and Pork

3 ounces canned bamboo
  shoots, rinsed and drained
3 ounces fresh spinach,
  cleaned and trimmed
1/8 ounce dried cloud ears,
  softened and cleaned
6 ounces boneless pork
  shoulder
4 teaspoons rice wine
3½ teaspoons cornstarch
1 teaspoon sesame oil
2 tablespoons cold water
1½ tablespoons soy sauce
1 tablespoon Chinese black
  vinegar
1½ teaspoons sugar
5 large eggs
5 tablespoons peanut oil
3 tablespoons finely chopped
  green onion
2 teaspoons minced pared
  fresh ginger root
1 clove garlic, minced
½ to 1 teaspoon chili sauce
  with soy bean

spinach leaves crosswise into 2-inch pieces. Break cloud ears into 1-inch pieces.

1. Cut bamboo shoots into 1/16-inch thick slices; cut slices into 2×1-inch pieces. Cut

2. Cut pork across the grain into 1/8-inch thick slices; cut slices into 2×1-inch pieces.

Combine pork and 1½ teaspoons rice wine in small bowl. Stir in 1½ teaspoons cornstarch; mix well. Stir in sesame oil. Marinate at room temperature 30 minutes.

3. Mix 2 teaspoons cornstarch and the cold water in cup until smooth; stir in soy sauce, vinegar, sugar and 2½ teaspoons rice wine. Beat eggs in medium bowl.

4. Heat wok over high heat 15 seconds; add 2 tablespoons peanut oil and heat until hot, about 30 seconds. Add eggs; quickly swirl around wok. As eggs begin to puff at edges, push cooked portion to one side, tilting wok in opposite direction, letting uncooked portion flow down. Repeat until eggs are set, not hard. (Work quickly; total cooking time for eggs is about 20 seconds.) Transfer to plate. Chop eggs with spatula into ½-inch wide strips.

5. Add 3 tablespoons peanut oil to wok; heat over high heat until hot. Scatter in pork; stir-fry until no longer pink, 1 minute. Add onion, ginger and garlic; stir-fry 10 seconds. Stir in chili sauce; stir-fry 5 seconds. Add cloud ears and bamboo shoots; stir-fry 30 seconds.

6. Stir soy sauce mixture; add to wok. Cook and stir until thickened, 15 seconds. Stir in spinach. Add eggs; cook and stir until eggs are heated through, about 10 seconds.
Makes 3 to 4 servings

Seasoned Fish and Bean Curd

¾ pound skinless firm white
  fish fillets, such as cod,
  haddock or sea bass
2½ tablespoons rice wine
¼ teaspoon salt
1 large egg white, lightly
  beaten
3 tablespoons cornstarch
1 pound bean curd
1¼ cups chicken stock or
  broth
2 tablespoons soy sauce
2 teaspoons Chinese black
  vinegar
2 teaspoons sugar
1 teaspoon sesame oil
2 tablespoons cold water
3 cups vegetable oil
3 tablespoons peanut oil
2 teaspoons minced pared
  fresh ginger root
1 clove garlic, minced
1 to 2 teaspoons chili paste
  with garlic
3 tablespoons finely chopped
  green onion

1. Cut fish crosswise into ½-inch wide strips; cut strips into 1½-inch lengths. Combine fish, 1 tablespoon rice wine and the salt in medium bowl. Stir in egg white. Sprinkle with 5 teaspoons cornstarch; stir until smooth. Refrigerate, covered, 30 minutes to 1 hour.

2. Cut bean curd into 3/8-inch thick slices; cut slices into 2×¾-inch pieces. Mix chicken stock, soy sauce, vinegar, sugar, sesame oil and 1½ tablespoons rice wine in small bowl. Mix 4 teaspoons corn-

starch with the water in a cup until smooth.

3. Heat wok over high heat 20 seconds; add vegetable oil to wok and heat to 325°F. Stir fish to separate. Fry fish, ½ at a time, just until cooked through, 1½ to 2 minutes. Remove with strainer; drain on paper toweling. Reheat oil to 325°F and repeat with remaining fish. Remove oil from wok; wipe clean.

4. Heat large saucepan of water to boiling. Add bean curd. Heat to boiling; reduce heat to low. Simmer bean curd 2 minutes; drain thoroughly.

5. Heat wok over high heat 15 seconds; add peanut oil and heat until hot, about 30 seconds. Reduce heat to medium; stir-fry ginger and garlic 10 seconds. Stir in chili paste; stir-fry 5 seconds. Add stock mixture, bean curd and green onion.

6. Increase heat to high; heat to boiling. Reduce heat to medium-low; simmer uncovered, stirring gently, 4 minutes. Stir in fish; simmer and stir 1 minute. Quickly stir cornstarch mixture and add to wok; cook and stir gently until sauce thickens and coats ingredients, 30 to 45 seconds. Serve immediately.
Makes 4 servings

Custard with Chicken and Shrimp

2 thin slices fresh ginger root
3 tablespoons rice wine
6 fresh medium shrimp,
    shelled and deveined
3 ounces skinless boneless
    chicken breast
5 large egg whites
2 tablespoons cornstarch
3½ tablespoons peanut oil
1½ ounces canned bamboo
    shoots, rinsed and drained
3 medium dried black
    Chinese mushrooms,
    softened and cleaned
Boiling water
3 cups chicken stock or broth
1 teaspoon salt
Pinch white pepper
2½ tablespoons cold water
3 tablespoons frozen peas,
    thawed and drained

1. Pare ginger root; pound lightly with flat side of cleaver. Combine with ½ tablespoon rice wine in small bowl.

2. Butterfly shrimp: Cut along outside curve, ¾ through body; cut crosswise in half. Slant-cut chicken across grain

into ⅛-inch thick slices; stack slices and cut into 1¼-inch pieces. Stir chicken and shrimp into rice wine mixture.

3. Lightly beat egg whites; add 1 tablespoon to chicken mixture. Stir to mix well. Reserve remaining whites. Stir ½ tablespoon cornstarch into chicken; mix well. Drizzle with ½ tablespoon oil; mix well. Refrigerate, covered, 30 minutes. Cut bamboo shoots into ⅛-inch thick slices; cut slices into 1½×1-inch pieces. Slant-cut mushrooms crosswise into 4 slices each.

4. Stir 1 tablespoon peanut oil into 1 quart boiling water in wok; reduce heat to medium. Stir chicken mixture; discard ginger. Add chicken mixture to wok; stir gently. Cook until coating turns white, 30 to 45 seconds; drain in sieve.

5. Add 1½ cups stock, 1 tablespoon rice wine, ½ teaspoon salt and the pepper to reserved egg whites; stir to mix well. Divide among 4 heat-proof bowls, 1½- to 2-cup size; cover with foil.*

6. Place bowls in steamer basket (2 steamers can be used); cover. Place steamer in wok; add boiling water to wok to level of 1 inch below steamer. Adjust heat for gentle steady steam, about medium. Steam custard until knife inserted in center is withdrawn clean, 10 to 15 minutes. Remove basket from wok; empty wok and wipe dry.

7. Mix 1½ cups stock, 1½ tablespoons rice wine and ½ teaspoon salt in small bowl. Mix 1½ tablespoons cornstarch and the cold water in a cup until smooth.

8. Heat wok over high heat 15 seconds; add 2 tablespoons oil and heat until hot, about 30 seconds. Add bamboo shoots; stir-fry 30 seconds. Add mushrooms; stir-fry 30 seconds. Add chicken and shrimp; stir-fry 30 seconds. Add peas; stir-fry 15 seconds. Add stock mixture; heat to boiling. Stir cornstarch mixture; add to wok. Cook and stir until sauce thickens, 30 seconds. Ladle sauce over custards, dividing evenly. Serve immediately.

Makes 4 servings

Or use lightly oiled bowl, 8½×2 inches; steam 15 to 20 minutes.

Eggs with Chinese Chives

1 small cucumber (for
    garnish)
¼ cup cornstarch
¼ cup cold water
6 large eggs
1 cup chicken stock or broth
⅓ cup Chinese chives, cut in
    1-inch lengths*
¾ teaspoon salt
⅛ teaspoon pepper
5 tablespoons peanut oil

If Chinese chives are unavailable, substitute regular chives or green onion tops plus ¼ teaspoon minced garlic.

1. For cucumber garnish, follow directions in Step 3 of "Batter-Fried Shrimp" (see Index for page number).

2. Mix cornstarch and cold water in a cup until smooth. Beat eggs in medium bowl; whisk in stock and cornstarch mixture until thoroughly mixed. Stir in chives, salt and pepper.

3. Heat wok over high heat 15 seconds; add 3 tablespoons oil and heat until hot, about 30 seconds. Add egg mixture and quickly swirl around wok. As

eggs begin to set on bottom, push cooked portion to one side, tilting wok in opposite direction and letting uncooked portion flow down; repeat until eggs are ¾ cooked. Push egg mixture to center of wok.

4. Add 1 tablespoon oil to wok, pouring it in a circle around edge of eggs. Lift egg mixture in several places, letting oil flow underneath. Spread eggs in even layer. Reduce heat to low; cook, covered, until bottom is golden, 3 to 5 minutes.

5. Cut egg mixture into 3 or 4 pieces with spatula and turn. Add 1 tablespoon oil around edge and lift eggs as in Step 4. Cook, covered, until golden, 3 to 5 minutes longer. Transfer to cutting board.

6. Cut egg mixture lengthwise in thirds; cut crosswise into 1-inch wide pieces. Arrange eggs and cucumber garnish on heated serving dish. Serve immediately.

Makes 3 or 4 servings

Vegetables

Tangy Marinated Cucumbers

1 pound cucumbers,
   preferably unwaxed
   (about 2 medium)
1 large clove garlic
3 tablespoons peanut oil
1 or 2 dried red chili peppers
1 tablespoon soy sauce
2 tablespoons sugar
½ teaspoon salt
1 piece (2×½×½-inches)
   fresh ginger root, pared
1 fresh red or green chili
   pepper, seeded
1 tablespoon sesame oil
½ teaspoon zanthoxylum
   seeds or ¼ teaspoon
   Szechuan peppercorns
2 tablespoons distilled white
   vinegar

1. Cut cucumbers lengthwise into halves; scoop out and discard seeds. Cut halves lengthwise into ¾- to 1-inch wide strips; cut strips crosswise into 2 to 2½-inch lengths. Place pieces cut-side-down on paper toweling. Pound garlic clove lightly with flat side of cleaver.

2. Heat wok over high heat 15 seconds; add peanut oil and heat until hot, about 30 seconds. Reduce heat to low. Add garlic and dried chili peppers; cook, stirring and pressing against wok until peppers are dark red but not burned, about 10 seconds.

3. Increase heat to high. Scatter in cucumbers; stir-fry until skin is bright green, about 30 seconds. Drizzle with soy sauce and sprinkle with sugar; stir-fry until sugar melts, about 5 seconds. Do not let it burn. Immediately transfer mixture to heatproof bowl. Sprinkle with salt; stir. Refrigerate covered, stirring occasionally, until cucumbers are well chilled, about 4 hours.

4. Cut ginger lengthwise into ¹/₁₆-inch thick slices; stack slices overlapping slightly and cut lengthwise into ¹/₁₆-inch wide shreds. Cut fresh chili pepper lengthwise into ¹/₁₆-inch wide shreds.

5. Heat wok over high heat 15 seconds; reduce heat to medium. Add sesame oil; heat until hot, about 15 seconds. Add zanthoxylum seeds; stir-fry until fragrant, about 5 seconds. Add ginger and fresh chili pepper; stir-fry 30 seconds. Transfer mixture to plate.

6. Remove garlic and dried chili peppers from cucumbers; discard. Stir vinegar into cucumbers. Arrange cucumbers on serving dish; pour about half the dressing over them. Arrange ginger mixture on top of cucumbers. Serve immediately.

Makes 3 to 4 servings

Stuffed Eggplant Slices

6 ounces ground pork or beef, march-chopped

4 tablespoons minced green onion, white part only

2 tablespoons plus 2 teaspoons soy sauce

1 small egg yolk

¼ teaspoon salt

Pinch pepper

⅔ cup plus 1 tablespoon plus 2 teaspoons cornstarch

⅔ cup plus 1 tablespoon cold water

1 small egg, beaten

1 cup all-purpose flour

¼ cup rice vinegar

¼ cup sugar

2 tablespoons rice wine

1 tablespoon minced pared fresh ginger root

1½ pounds Chinese eggplants*

5 cups vegetable oil

1 tablespoon peanut oil

If unavailable, select eggplants 2 inches or less in diameter.

1. Combine pork, 2 tablespoons onion, 2 teaspoons soy sauce, the egg yolk, salt and pepper; mix thoroughly. Stir in 1 tablespoon cornstarch; mix well.

2. Mix ⅓ cup cornstarch and ⅔ cup water until smooth. Whisk in egg; whisk in flour until batter is smooth.

3. Mix 2 teaspoons cornstarch and 1 tablespoon cold water until smooth. Add vinegar, sugar, rice wine, ginger, 2 tablespoons soy sauce and 2 tablespoons onion; stir until sugar dissolves.

4. Pare eggplant. Slice eggplant crosswise at ¼-inch intervals, cutting only ¾ through on first slice and cutting completely through on second slice.

5. Brush the pockets in eggplant slices lightly with part of the ⅓ cup cornstarch. Divide meat mixture evenly among pockets; press eggplant slices together lightly. Roll eggplant in remaining cornstarch to coat outer surfaces; brush off excess. Place in single layer on plate.

6. Heat wok over high heat 20 seconds; add vegetable oil and heat to 350°F. Reduce heat to medium. Hold eggplant by uncut edge; dip into batter to coat. Add to wok. Fry 6 to 8 pieces at a time; stir gently and turn occasionally, until pale golden, 2½ to 3½ minutes. Remove with strainer; drain on paper toweling.

7. When eggplant is fried, heat oil over high heat to 375°F; reduce heat to medium. Fry eggplant again, ½ at a time, until deep golden and crisp, 1½ to 2 minutes. Remove with strainer; drain on paper toweling. Remove oil from wok; wipe clean.

8. Heat wok over high heat 15 seconds; add peanut oil and heat until hot, about 30 seconds. Add vinegar mixture; cook and stir until sauce thickens, about 30 seconds. Add eggplant; stir and fold 2 or 3 times to coat with sauce. Serve immediately.

Makes 4 to 5 servings

Green Beans in Spicy Sauce

8 ounces boneless pork loin, end cut

1½ cups chicken stock or broth

2 tablespoons soy sauce

1 tablespoon rice wine

1 teaspoon sugar

2 teaspoons cornstarch

1½ tablespoons cold water

2 cups vegetable oil

1 pound fresh green beans

3 tablespoons peanut oil

2 tablespoons minced green onion, white part only

2 teaspoons minced pared fresh ginger root

1 medium clove garlic, minced

1 or 2 dried red chili peppers, seeded

2 teaspoons cider vinegar

1. To facilitate slicing, freeze pork until firm but not frozen, 20 to 30 minutes. Cut pork across the grain into ⅛-inch thick slices; cut slices into 2¼×½-inch strips.

2. Mix chicken stock, soy sauce, rice wine and sugar in small bowl until sugar dissolves. Mix cornstarch and cold water in a cup until smooth.

3. Heat wok over high heat 20 seconds; add vegetable oil and heat to 375°F. Add beans, about ¼ at a time; fry, stirring constantly, until beans are slightly wrinkled, about 3 minutes after all beans are added. Remove beans with strainer; drain on paper toweling. Remove oil from wok; wipe clean.

4. Heat wok over high heat 15 seconds; add peanut oil and heat until hot, about 30 seconds. Reduce heat to medium. Add onion, ginger and garlic; stir-fry 10 seconds.

5. Increase heat to high. Scatter in pork; stir-fry until pork is no longer pink, about 1½

minutes. Add chili peppers and stock mixture. Heat to boiling. Reduce heat to medium; cook, covered, 2 minutes.

6. Add beans to wok; increase heat to high. Heat to boiling; reduce heat to medium-low. Simmer, uncovered, stirring constantly and flipping beans over, 4 minutes. Stir cornstarch mixture and add to wok; cook and stir until sauce is thickened, about 45 seconds. Drizzle with vinegar; stir 2 or 3 times.

Makes 3 to 4 servings

Bean Sprouts with Shredded Pork

8 ounces boneless pork loin blade, or beef flank steak
2 tablespoons rice wine
¾ teaspoon salt
Pinch black pepper
1 small egg, lightly beaten
1 tablespoon cornstarch
6 tablespoons plus 2 teaspoons peanut oil
1 pound fresh mung bean sprouts
2 quarts boiling water
1 bunch (about 4 ounces) Chinese chives
3 green onions, white part only
1 to 2 dried red chili peppers, seeded
1 large clove garlic
1 tablespoon minced pared fresh ginger root
1 tablespoon soy sauce

1. To facilitate slicing, freeze pork until firm but not frozen, 20 to 30 minutes. Cut pork across the grain into ⅛-inch thick slices. Stack slices, slightly overlapping, and cut lengthwise into ⅛-inch wide shreds.

2. Combine pork shreds, 1 tablespoon rice wine, ¼ teaspoon salt and the black pepper in small bowl; stir in egg. Sprinkle with cornstarch; stir to mix well. Stir in 2 teaspoons oil; refrigerate, covered, 30 minutes.

3. Place sprouts in bowl of cold water; skim off and discard green husks and broken tips that float to surface. Drain sprouts. Add to boiling water in large saucepan; cook over high heat 30 seconds. Drain; plunge into bowl of cold water. Drain well; pat dry with paper toweling.

4. Rinse chives; cut off and discard tough root ends. Pat

dry. Cut chives into 2½-inch lengths. Cut onions crosswise into ¼-inch pieces. Cut chili peppers into ½-inch pieces. Pound garlic lightly with flat side of cleaver.

5. Heat wok over high heat 15 seconds; add 3 tablespoons oil and heat until hot, about 30 seconds. Stir pork; remove from egg mixture with slotted spoon, draining well. Discard egg mixture. Add pork to wok, ⅓ at a time; stir-fry until no longer pink, about 2 minutes after all pork is added. Transfer to plate.

6. Add 3 tablespoons oil to wok; heat until hot. Reduce heat to low. Add chili pepper and garlic; stir-fry until pepper is dark red, about 10 seconds. Add onion and ginger; stir-fry 10 seconds. Increase heat to high. Scatter in sprouts, ¼ at a time; stir-fry 30 seconds after all sprouts are

added. Add chives and ½ teaspoon salt; stir-fry 30 seconds. Add pork and 1 tablespoon rice wine; stir-fry 1 minute. Drizzle with soy sauce; stir 2 or 3 times. Discard garlic. Serve immediately.
Makes 4 servings

Simmered Turnip and Carrot Balls

1 cup boiling water
1 ounce dried scallops
1 pound fresh Chinese turnip, pared
¾ pound carrots (about 1-inch diameter), pared
4 thin slices fresh ginger root, pared
2 green onions
1½ cups vegetable oil
1½ cups chicken stock or broth
2 tablespoons lard
2 tablespoons rice wine
1 tablespoon soy sauce
1 teaspoon sugar
Pinch pepper
2 teaspoons cornstarch
1 tablespoon cold water

1. Pour boiling water over scallops in small bowl; soak 30 minutes.

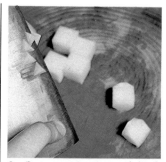

2. Cut turnip into 1-inch cubes. If desired, cut off corners of each cube at an angle.

3. Cut carrots crosswise into ¾-inch thick rounds. Remove edges on top and bottom of

carrot pieces to give rounded shape. Pound ginger and onions lightly with flat side of cleaver.

4. Heat wok over high heat 20 seconds; add oil to wok and heat to 325°F. Fry carrots, stirring occasionally, until evenly

covered with yellowish film, 2 to 2½ minutes. Remove with strainer; drain on paper toweling. Remove oil from wok; wipe clean.

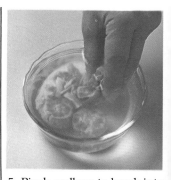

5. Pinch scallops to break into shreds; rinse well.

6. Combine turnip, carrots, scallops, onions and ginger in wok. Add stock, lard, rice wine, soy sauce, sugar and pepper. Heat to boiling; reduce heat to medium-low. Cook, covered, until vegetables are tender, about 20 minutes. Remove and discard onions and ginger. Mix cornstarch and cold water in a cup until smooth. Add to wok; cook and stir until sauce thickens, about 45 seconds.
Makes 3 to 4 servings

Asparagus in Crab Sauce

1 pound fresh asparagus
3 or 4 large lettuce leaves
Boiling water
6 ounces fresh or thawed
   frozen crab meat
1 tablespoon rice wine
1 cup chicken stock or broth
1 tablespoon soy sauce
½ teaspoon sugar
½ teaspoon salt
1 tablespoon cornstarch
2 tablespoons cold water
3 tablespoons peanut oil
2 tablespoons finely chopped
   green onion
1 teaspoon minced pared
   fresh ginger root

1. Cut off asparagus tips. If stalks are thicker than ½ inch diameter, cut lengthwise in half. Cut stalks crosswise into 1½-inch lengths.

2. Line steamer basket with lettuce leaves; spread asparagus tips and stalks on lettuce. Place steamer in wok. Cover steamer. Add boiling water to wok to level of 1 inch below steamer. Cover wok; steam asparagus over boiling water until crisp-tender, 5 to 7 minutes.

3. Break crab meat into coarse shreds, removing any bits of shell or cartilage. Combine crab and rice wine in small bowl. Mix stock, soy sauce, sugar and salt in second small bowl. Mix cornstarch and cold water in a cup until smooth.

4. When asparagus is cooked, remove steamer from wok. Transfer asparagus to plate; discard lettuce. Discard water; wipe wok dry.

5. Heat wok over high heat 15 seconds; add oil and heat until hot, about 30 seconds. Reduce heat to medium. Add onion and ginger; stir-fry 10 seconds. Add crab; stir-fry 15 seconds. Stir in asparagus; increase heat to high. Add stock mixture; heat to boiling. Cover wok; steam-cook asparagus mixture 30 seconds. Uncover wok. Stir cornstarch mixture and add to wok; cook and stir until sauce is thickened, about 30 seconds. Serve immediately.

Makes 3 to 4 servings

Hot and Spicy Shredded Cabbage

2 pounds napa (preferably
   near root end)
2 tablespoons salt
¼ cup water
1 piece pared fresh ginger
   root, 2×1¼×1¼ inches
1 to 3 dried red chili peppers
2 tablespoons sugar
2 tablespoons distilled white
   vinegar
1 tablespoon soy sauce
3 tablespoons peanut oil
1 tablespoon sesame oil

1. Separate cabbage leaves; cut crosswise into 4-inch lengths. Stack a few leaves at a time and cut lengthwise into ³⁄₁₆-inch wide shreds. Place cabbage in large bowl; sprinkle with salt and toss. Drizzle with water. Top cabbage with a plate and 3-pound weight, such as canned goods. Let stand 30 minutes.

2. Cut ginger lengthwise into ¹⁄₁₆-inch thick slices; stack slices and cut lengthwise into ¹⁄₁₆-inch wide shreds. Cut chili peppers crosswise with scissors into ⅛-inch pieces; remove and discard seeds.

3. Rinse cabbage thoroughly in large bowl of cold water, changing water several times; drain well. Squeeze cabbage between several layers of paper toweling to remove excess water.

4. Combine cabbage, ginger and chili pepper in large bowl. Add sugar, vinegar and soy sauce; stir to mix well.

5. Heat wok over high heat 15 seconds. Add peanut and sesame oils and heat until hot, about 30 seconds. Add cabbage mixture; heat to boiling. Reduce heat to medium-low. Simmer, covered, stirring occasionally, just until cabbage is crisp-tender, about 5 minutes. Uncover wok; increase heat to high. Cook, stirring constantly and rapidly, 2 minutes. Serve hot. Or refrigerate, covered, until cold; remove cabbage from liquid with slotted spoon and serve.

Makes 3 to 4 servings

Vegetable Stir-Fry

2 ounces Chinese pickled
    cabbage
½ cup shelled fresh peas or
    thawed frozen peas
Boiling water
3 medium green bell peppers
1 ounce canned bamboo
    shoots, rinsed and drained
3 tablespoons peanut oil
2 tablespoons finely chopped
    green onion, white part
    only
1 teaspoon minced pared
    fresh ginger root
1 tablespoon soy sauce
1 tablespoon rice wine
1 teaspoon sugar

1. Soak cabbage in bowl of cold water 10 minutes; drain well. If not already shredded, cut cabbage into ⅛-inch wide shreds. Squeeze dry between paper toweling.

2. If using fresh peas, add to small saucepan of boiling water; cook 1 minute. Rinse under cold water to cool; drain well.

3. Cut green peppers lengthwise into 3/16-inch wide strips. Cut bamboo shoots lengthwise into ⅛-inch thick slices. Stack slices and cut lengthwise into 1/16-inch wide shreds; cut shreds crosswise into 1½-inch lengths.

4. Heat wok over high heat 15 seconds; add oil and heat until hot, about 30 seconds. Reduce heat to medium. Add onion and ginger; stir-fry 10 seconds. Increase heat to high. Add bamboo shoots; stir-fry

30 seconds. Add cabbage; stir-fry 30 seconds. Scatter in peppers, ⅓ at a time; stir-fry 2 minutes after all peppers are added. Add peas; stir-fry 30 seconds. Add soy sauce, rice wine and sugar. Cook and stir 15 seconds. Serve immediately.

Makes 3 to 4 servings

Hot and Sour Cucumbers

1¼ pounds very thin
    cucumbers*
1 tablespoon salt
¼ cup plus 1½ tablespoons
    cold water
2 green onions, white part
    only
1 to 3 dried red chili peppers,
    seeded
1 large clove garlic
1 tablespoon cornstarch
2 tablespoons chicken stock
    or broth
2 tablespoons Chinese black
    vinegar
1 tablespoon soy sauce
1 tablespoon rice wine
1 tablespoon sugar
4 tablespoons peanut oil

Use the long thin waxless cucumbers, about 1-inch in diameter, found in Oriental grocery stores. If unavailable, use "seedless" cucumbers.

1. Slant-cut cucumbers at ⅛-inch intervals, leaving slices attached ⅜-inch from bottom on first 3 cuts; cut through to detach piece on fourth cut. (If cucumbers are larger than 1¼ inches in diameter, cut pieces lengthwise in half.) Place cucumbers in medium bowl; sprinkle with salt and toss. Drizzle with ¼ cup water. Top cucumbers with a plate and 3-pound weight, such as canned goods; let stand 10 minutes.

2. Cut onions crosswise into ½-inch pieces. Cut chili peppers crosswise into ½-inch pieces. Pound garlic lightly with flat side of cleaver.

3. Mix cornstarch and 1½ tablespoons cold water until smooth; stir in chicken stock, vinegar, soy sauce, rice wine and sugar until sugar dissolves.

4. Rinse cucumbers thoroughly in sieve under cold running water; drain well. Pat dry between several layers of paper toweling.

5. Heat wok over high heat 15 seconds; add 3 tablespoons oil and heat until hot, about 30 seconds. Reduce heat to low. Add chili pepper and garlic; stir-fry until pepper is dark red, about 10 seconds. Add onion; stir-fry 10 seconds. Increase heat to high. Scatter in cucumbers, ¼ at a time; stir-

fry until crisp-tender, about 3 minutes after all cucumbers are added. Stir cornstarch mixture and add to wok; cook and stir until thickened, about 30 seconds. Drizzle with 1 tablespoon oil; stir 2 or 3 times. Discard garlic. Serve immediately.

Makes 4 servings

Napa in Cream Sauce

2 medium heads napa (about
2½ pounds each)
1 can (3½ ounces) whole
button mushrooms,
drained
3 ounces Canadian bacon or
ham
2 tablespoons lard
1 cup chicken stock or broth
1 tablespoon rice wine
¾ teaspoon salt
½ teaspoon sugar
⅛ teaspoon white pepper
1 tablespoon plus 1 teaspoon
cornstarch
2 tablespoons cold water
¼ cup whipping cream
2 tablespoons peanut oil

1. Peel off outer leaves of napa
to reach yellow-white inner
leaves (napa heart will be 3
inches in diameter). Cut off
tops 5 to 5½ inches from base.
(Save outer leaves and tops
for other uses.) Starting about
½ inch from base of napa

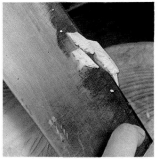

heart, trim base by diagonally
shaving off thin slices; do not
detach any leaves.

2. Cut each napa lengthwise
into 4 equal wedges. Insert
blade diagonally into base of

each wedge and cut to separate into 2 pieces, leaving 2 or
3 leaves in the outer piece. Cut
outer pieces of napa lengthwise in thirds. Cut inner
pieces lengthwise in half.

3. Cut mushrooms crosswise
into ⅛-inch thick slices. Cut
bacon crosswise into ⅛-inch
thick slices; stack slices and
cut into 4 wedges.

4. Heat wok over high heat 15
seconds; add lard; heat until
melted and hot, about 30 seconds. Add bacon; stir-fry 1
minute; transfer bacon with
slotted spoon to plate. Add
stock and rice wine to wok.
Arrange napa in wok in even
layer. Heat to boiling; adjust
heat to maintain low simmer.
Simmer covered until napa is
tender, 6 to 8 minutes. Do not
uncover during cooking;
gently tilt and shake wok occasionally to prevent napa
from sticking.

5. Add mushrooms and bacon
to wok; sprinkle in salt, sugar
and pepper. Stir gently. Mix
cornstarch and cold water in a
cup until smooth; pour
around edge of liquid in wok.

Increase heat to high; cook
and stir gently until sauce
thickens, about 30 seconds.
Reduce heat to very low. Pour
cream and oil around edge of
liquid in wok; stir in gently.
Cook just until oil floats to
top, 10 to 15 seconds. Gently
ladle into heated serving
bowl. Serve immediately.
Makes 4 servings

Spicy Eggplant

1 pound eggplant (preferably
thin)
6 ounces boneless pork
shoulder
8 to 10 green onions, white
part only
2 tablespoons soy sauce
1½ tablespoons ground
brown bean sauce
1 tablespoon rice wine
1 tablespoon Chinese black
vinegar
1 tablespoon sugar
2 teaspoons chili sauce with
soy bean
4 cups vegetable oil
2 tablespoons peanut oil
2 teaspoons minced pared
fresh ginger root
1 clove garlic, minced

1. Pare ½-inch wide strips of
skin lengthwise at ½-inch
intervals around eggplant.
Cut eggplant lengthwise into
1-inch wide wedges; cut
wedges into 3-inch lengths.
Place eggplant in bowl with
cold water to cover.

2. Cut pork across the grain
into ⅛-inch thick slices; cut
slices into 2×1-inch pieces.
Cut onions into 1½-inch
lengths.

3. Mix soy sauce, bean sauce,
rice wine, vinegar, sugar and
chili sauce in small bowl.

4. Heat wok over high heat 20
seconds; add vegetable oil and
heat to 375°F. Drain eggplant;
pat dry with paper toweling.
Fry eggplant, ½ at a time,
until golden and just barely
tender, 1½ to 2 minutes. Remove eggplant with strainer;
drain on paper toweling.
Gently blot with more paper
toweling. Remove oil from
wok; wipe clean.

5. Heat wok over high heat 15
seconds; add peanut oil and
heat until hot, about 30 seconds. Stir-fry onions 1 min-

ute; remove with slotted
spoon to plate.

6. Stir-fry pork in oil remaining in wok 1 minute. Push
pork to side; reduce heat to
medium. Stir-fry ginger and
garlic 10 seconds; then mix in
pork. Increase heat to high.

Stir in soy sauce mixture. Return onions to wok. Cook and
stir until sauce thickens
slightly, about 1 minute. Stir
in eggplant; stir and toss until
coated with sauce and heated
through, about 30 seconds.
Makes 3 to 4 servings

Curry Fried Rice

½ pound fresh small shrimp, shelled and deveined
1 tablespoon rice wine
1½ teaspoons cornstarch
⅓ cup fresh peas*
Boiling water
4 medium dried black Chinese mushrooms, softened and cleaned
6 tablespoons peanut oil
1 medium yellow onion, chopped
1 to 3 tablespoons curry sauce
2 tablespoons soy sauce
½ teaspoon salt
3½ cups cooked rice, at room temperature**

*Frozen peas may be used. Thaw and drain well; omit boiling in Step 2.

**For best results, prepare rice several hours ahead; cool, uncovered, to room temperature.

1. Combine shrimp and rice wine in small bowl. Sprinkle with cornstarch; stir to mix well. Marinate at room temperature 20 minutes; drain.

2. Add peas to small saucepan of boiling water; cook 1 minute. Rinse under cold running water; drain well. Cut mushrooms into ½-inch pieces.

3. Heat wok over high heat 15 seconds; add 2 tablespoons oil and heat 10 seconds. Reduce heat to medium. Scatter in shrimp; stir-fry until cooked through, about 1½ minutes. Transfer shimp to plate.

4. Add 1 tablespoon oil to wok; heat over high heat 10 seconds. Reduce heat to low. Add mushrooms; stir-fry 1½ minutes. Transfer to bowl.

5. Add 3 tablespoons oil to wok; heat over high heat 30 seconds. Add onion; stir-fry until translucent, about 1 minute. Add curry sauce; stir-fry 30 seconds. Stir in soy sauce, salt and mushrooms; reduce heat to medium. Add

rice; stir-fry, tossing and poking at rice to separate grains, until heated through and uniform in color, about 2 minutes.

6. Add shrimp and peas rice; stir-fry 30 seconds. Serv immediately.

Makes 4 to 6 serving

Conversion Charts

METRIC EQUIVALENTS FOR U.S. VOLUME MEASURES

.S. Volume Measure	Metric Equivalent
/8 teaspoon	0.5 milliliter
/4 teaspoon	1 milliliter
/2 teaspoon	2 milliliters
teaspoon	5 milliliters
/2 tablespoon	7 milliliters
tablespoon (3 teaspoons)	15 milliliters
tablespoons (1 fluid ounce)	30 milliliters
/4 cup (4 tablespoons)	60 milliliters
/3 cup	80 milliliters
/2 cup (4 fluid ounces)	125 milliliters
/3 cup	160 milliliters
/4 cup (6 fluid ounces)	180 milliliters
cup (16 tablespoons)	250 milliliters
pint (2 cups)	500 milliliters
quart (4 cups)	1 Liter

METRIC EQUIVALENTS FOR TEMPERATURES

Degrees ahrenheit	Degrees Celsius
00°F	100°C
50°F	120°C
75°F	140°C
00°F	150°C
25°F	160°C
50°F	180°C
75°F	190°C
00°F	200°C
25°F	220°C
50°F	230°C

METRIC EQUIVALENTS FOR U.S. WEIGHT MEASURES

U.S. Weight Measure	Metric Equivalent
½ ounce	15 grams
1 ounce	30 grams
2 ounces	60 grams
3 ounces	85 grams
¼ pound (4 ounces)	115 grams
½ pound (8 ounces)	225 grams
¾ pound (12 ounces)	340 grams
1 pound (16 ounces)	450 grams

METRIC EQUIVALENTS FOR U.S. DIMENSIONS

U.S. Dimension	Metric Equivalent
1/16 inch	2 millimeters
⅛ inch	3 millimeters
3/16 inch	5 millimeters
¼ inch	6 millimeters
⅜ inch	9 millimeters
½ inch	1.3 centimeters
⅝ inch	1.6 centimeters
¾ inch	1.9 centimeters
1 inch	2.5 centimeters
1½ inches	4 centimeters
2 inches	5 centimeters
3 inches	8 centimeters
4 inches	10 centimeters
5 inches	13 centimeters
9 inches	23 centimeters
11 inches	28 centimeters
13 inches	33 centimeters

ote: All metric equivalents are approximate; they have been rounded to the nearest metric equivalent or ease of use.

BRITISH IMPERIAL EQUIVALENTS FOR U.S. VOLUME MEASURES

U.S. Volume Measure	Imperial Equivalent
1 fluid ounce	1.04 fluid ounces
1 pint	0.83 pint
1 quart	0.83 quart
1 gallon	0.83 gallon

Index